Library of
Davidson College

Legal Almanac Series No. 66

LEGAL PROTECTION
IN
GARNISHMENT AND ATTACHMENT

By

Stanley Morganstern, B.S., J.D.
Member of the Ohio Bar Association

1971
OCEANA PUBLICATIONS, INC.
Dobbs Ferry, New York

This is the sixty-sixth number in a series of LEGAL ALMANACS which bring you the law on various subjects in nontechnical language. These books do not take the place of your attorney's advice, but they can introduce you to your legal rights and responsibilities.

347.73
M849ℓ

Library of Congress Catalog Card Number: 75-156376

International Standard Book Number: 0-379-11074-1

© Copyright 1971 by Oceana Publications, Inc.

Manufactured in the United States of America

82-7151

TABLE OF CONTENTS

Introduction v

Chapter I
BASIC LEGAL ASPECTS
   Garnishments 1
   Attachments 4
   Exemptions 5

Chapter II
GARNISHMENTS
   Garnishment of Wages before Judgment 7
   Garnishment of Wages after Judgment 10
   Pay Periods 17
   Chart 1 - Primary Features of State Exemption Statutes . 19
   Procedure 26
   Discharge from Employment 28
   Assignment of Wages 32
   Chart II - Wage Assignments (by State) 33
   State Exemptions from Federal Law 40
   Wage Exemptions 44
   Scope of Uniform Credit Code 46
   Recap of Wage Garnishments 46

Chapter III
GARNISHMENT -- OTHER THAN WAGES
   Generally 48
   Real Property 48
   Bank Accounts 49
   Life Insurance 51
   Chart III - Insurance Exemptions 53
   Partnership Property 59
   Equitable Interests 60

(Contents - continued)

GARNISHMENT -- OTHER THAN WAGES (cont'd.)
- Decedent's Estates 62
- Stock 63
- Pensions 63

Chapter IV
GARNISHMENT PROCEDURE 64

Chapter V
ATTACHMENT
- Generally 68
- Chart IV - Grounds for Attachment - State Statutes 70
- Constitutionality 90
- Grounds 91
- Levy of Attachment 96
- Wrongful Attachment 97

Chapter VI
EXEMPTIONS FROM ATTACHMENT
- Generally 100
- Legal Aspects 101
- Homstead Exemption 104
- Personal Property Exemptions 106
- Tools and Implements 107
- Household Goods and Wearing Apparel 108
- Miscellaneous Features 110

Chapter VII
CONCLUSION 112

Appendix A - The Consumer Credit Protection Act 115

Appendix B - Federal Wage Garnishment Notice to be
            Attached to Garnishment Order 117

Index 119

INTRODUCTION

According to reports compiled by the Federal Reserve Board, consumer credit has increased from approximately $7,222,000 in 1939 to $113,231,000 in 1969 while installment credit has increased from $4,503,000 to $90,663,000 during the same period.

While these figures reflect a tremendous boon in our economy and a standard of living unparalleled anywhere and at any time, the extensive use of credit in installment buying and personal loans has led to a vast increase in personal bankruptcies, garnishments, attachments and other judicial process whereby a debtor's property and wages may be used to satisfy outstanding obligations.

There is currently Federal legislation (The Consumer Credit Protection Act), proposed uniform state legislation (Uniform Consumer Credit Code) and many individual state statutes which have been enacted for the purpose of protecting the consumer and borrower from financial disaster as a result of garnishments and attachments, which processes are the concern of this Almanac.

Perhaps the best explanation of the spirit of the Federal legislation was set forth by President Lyndon B. Johnson in his message to Congress of March 15, 1967:

> "While consumer credit has enjoyed phenomenal growth over the past 20 years, so have personal bankruptcies. Title II of your committee's bill, restricting the garnishment of wages, will relieve many consumers from the greatest single pressure, forcing wage earners into bankruptcies.
>
> "Hundreds of workers among the poor lose their jobs or most of their wages each year as a result of garnishment proceedings. In many cases, wages are garnished by unscrupulous merchants and lenders whose practices trap the unwitting workers.

"I am directing the Attorney General, in consultation with the Secretary of Labor and the Director of Economic Opportunity, to make a comprehensive study of the problem of wage garnishment and to recommend the steps that should be taken to protect the hard-earned wages and the jobs of those who need the income most." 1968 U.S. Code Congressional and Administrative News, House Report No. 1040.

The legislation referred to by President Johnson became a reality as part of the "Consumer Credit Protection Act" also known as "The Truth in Lending Act," or "Regulation Z." This legislation will be discussed herein in detail. Suffice it to say, at this point, that the garnishment provisions of that Act limit the amount of personal wages which can be taken and prohibit the discharge of an employee simply because of the fact that he has been garnished for any one indebtedness.

To emphasize the need for such legislation, the House Committee pointed out that the number of personal bankruptcies had increased from 18,000 in 1950 to 208,000 in the fiscal year ended June 30, 1967. It was noted that those states which severely restrict garnishment of personal wages had a much lower incident of personal bankruptcy than those states allowing garnishment.

"The limitations on the garnishment of wages adopted by your committee, while permitting the continued orderly payment of consumer debts, will relieve countless honest debtors driven by economic desperation from plunging into bankruptcy in order to preserve their employment and insure a continued means of payment for themselves and their families."

It has been estimated that in those states having lenient garnishment statutes personal bankruptcies ranged between two and three hundred per 100,000 population while those states having stringent garnishment statutes only experience between five and nine bankruptcies per 100,000 of population.

We are now in an age which can be called the "Consumer Protection Era." We have seen such Federal legislation as: Truth in Lending; Flammable Fabrics Act of 1967; Wholesale Meat Act of 1967; Partnership for Health Amendments of 1967; National Gas Pipeline Safety Act of 1967; and Medical Devices Safety Act of 1967, among others.

All of these and other acts are important to the consumer, but mean nothing unless the consumer basically understands or at least recognizes that his personal economic life may be affected by them.

Beyond the threat of bankruptcy generated by garnishment or attachment is the very real threat of discharge from employment. The United States Labor Department estimated that between July 1, 1969 and July 1, 1970, some 200,000 to 600,000 employees would lose their jobs as a result of garnishment of wages. This threat has been met by the Federal and State governments, and now such possibility has been reduced, although how effectively remains in doubt.

It is the intent and purpose of this Almanac to familiarize the reader with the Federal and general state statutes pertaining to attachments and garnishments which can and do affect his economic life. It is not our purpose to report all of the technical provisions of each particular state's statutes but rather to generate awareness of rights and obligations of a consumer and debtor.

Chapter One

BASIC LEGAL ASPECTS

Garnishments

Both garnishments and attachments can be legally characterized as processes by which a creditor collects, applies, or subjects personal property, real property, wages, or funds due to his debtor, to the debt owed him. The obligation giving rise to the attachment or garnishment need not be one arising out of personal loan or installment purchase, but rather can arise out of a tort action (personal injury, property damage, etc.) or any type of claim. Basically, any claim which is due from one person to another can be satisfied in whole or in part by the use of garnishment or attachment proceedings.

Excluding for the moment the use of attachment before judgment has been obtained in a court of law, let us consider the normal procedure which gives rise to a garnishment proceeding.

John Debtor purchases an automobile from his favorite local dealer. In order to complete the purchase, he fills out the necessary credit application revealing his place of employment, the existence of bank accounts, checking accounts, and other personal and real property. John makes a small downpayment on the automobile and executes a promissory or cognovit note for the balance. He promises to pay a specified amount per month for a stated number of months until the remainder is paid. The note which John signed also, normally, states that if a payment is missed, the entire balance becomes due and payable at once, and that John authorizes any attorney at law to confess a judgment against him in the amount then due, without notice of the action and without right of appeal.

For the sake of example, let us say that John has unwittingly overextended himself. He did not contemplate the reduction in overtime hours available to him or the extra medical bills. In any event, John cannot keep up with his car payments, and one day his car is repossessed by the bank or other financial institution that had extended credit directly to John or that had bought the note John signed on a discount basis from the automobile dealer.

The next thing John knows is that the car is being sold at public sale and that he will be expected to make up any deficiency existing between the amount owed at the time of sale and the sales price. Of course, after the sale, a deficiency is likely to exist as there are added costs to be covered such as repossession charges.

Subsequent to the sale, a judgment is obtained against John on the note for the deficiency, and he receives notice that the bank intends to garnish his wages as a means of collecting that deficiency. The bank may have already tied up and applied John's bank account to the deficiency, but unless John can satisfy the bank, his paycheck will be reduced in the allowable percentage.

The funds which his employer must, by law, withhold will be forwarded to the court and applied on the bank's judgment. John, in most likelihood, will be continuously garnished, as often as permitted by law, until the entire judgment, plus interest and court costs, has been satisfied, or until he loses his employment.

The foregoing is an example of the use of garnishment as it pertains to wages. Garnishment is, however, more extensive. Garnishment generally can be thought of as any process by which a creditor imposes a trust upon funds held by or owed by any person to the debtor for the benefit of the creditor.

The Prentice-Hall Encyclopedic Dictionary of Business Law defines garnishment as:

> "The action of a judgment creditor to compel a third party owing money to, or holding money for, a judgment debtor to pay the money to the creditor instead of to the debtor."

When a garnishment procedure has been instituted, the person, corporation, or firm holding the debtor's funds or owing him money must comply with the applicable statutes imposing upon him certain obligations. Most garnishment statutes require such person, the garnishee, to file an answer with the court out of which the garnishment order came, and to submit the funds to the court.

Failure to comply can result in the garnishee being liable to the creditor, even though he does not actually hold any funds. The garnishee might even find himself faced with a contempt of court action.

The particular responsibilities of an employer or other garnishee will be discussed later on in this article, but it should be understood at this point that garnishment is a proceeding involving third persons; that is, the proceeding attempts to make the garnishee a trustee or custodian of the debtor's funds for the benefit of the creditor.

It can be said that the proceeding amounts to a restraining order upon the garnishee prohibiting him from turning over funds to the debtor.

Garnishment proceedings are limited in some states to debts which have arisen out of contractual obligations, while some states permit its use for any type of obligation. Again, it must be remembered that the rules of each state differ and this Almanac does not seek to cover in detail each state's statutes.

The amount of exempted wages, notice requirements, obligations of garnishees, and when garnishment is available are only a few of the variances from state to state.

As mentioned previously, there have been attempts at creating a Uniform Consumer Credit Code which would standardize garnishment rules among the states. Such a code was approved by the American Bar Association but, as yet, has not been widely adopted by the states.

The Federal legislation which, of course, is controlling on the states is an attempt to bring some semblance of similarity between the garnishment laws of each of the several states. That statute, however, provides that each state may impose its own rules and regulations which will take precedence over the Federal legislation if those rules and regulations are substantially similar to or more restrictive than the Federal legislation.

What that statute provides, then, is that each state may impose tighter controls, larger wage exemptions, and greater employee protection than the Federal law; but until the adoption of a uniform code, there will, however, be no real standardization among the states.

Attachments

Neither the remedy of garnishment nor attachment was known at common law in the United States. In accordance with general legal principles, these statutory remedies must be strictly construed and generally in favor of the debtor.

While garnishment can be thought of as a remedy invoked after judgment, attachment usually pertains to a creditor's rights to seize, sequestor, or tie up the debtor's property prior to the creditor taking judgment against the debtor.

Although no one definition can cover all of the ramifications of attachment, The Prentice-Hall Encyclopedic Dictionary of Business Law defines attachment as:

> "The process by which a debtor's property (real property or personal property) is placed in the custody of the law and held as security pending the outcome of a creditor's suit. Until the case is decided, the debtor cannot dispose of his property or place it beyond the reach of the creditor. The most usual grounds for attachment are: (1) the debtor is a non-resident or a foreign corporation; (2) the debtor has left the state or is in hiding; (3) the debtor is about to remove, conceal, or dispose of his property."

As in the case of garnishments, the several states have enacted their own rules and regulations regarding attachments. There is no uniform act or controlling Federal legislation in this area; but in most of those states allowing attachment, the same general procedural rules apply.

Generally, a creditor wishing to attach a debtor's property prior to judgment must first begin by filing an affidavit stating: the amount of the claim; that the claim is a just one; that no part of the claim has been paid; that the debt was incurred in one of the particular ways enumerated in the statute; that the creditor is not indebted to the debtor (no setoffs); and that there are adequate grounds for attachment, as specified in the particular state's statute.

Contemporaneous with the filing of the affidavit, the creditor is usually required to file a bond which indemnifies the debtor in the event the attachment is wrongful.

After the appropriate documents have been filed, the sheriff or bailiff will levy execution on the property, making a return to the court as to the fact that the execution was made and the location and description of the property attached. Once the attachment has been made, the property is held pending final outcome of the primary suit by the creditor against the alleged debtor. Some states provide that the debtor may re-obtain his property and the use thereof by posting a redelivery bond.

A redelivery bond protects the creditor in that while the specific property attached is no longer subject to the creditor's claim, there is a fund out of which the creditor may satisfy his claim if he later obtains a judgment against the debtor.

Most jurisdictions view attachment upon property in advance of judgment as being a remedy available only under extraordinary circumstances where it appears that the creditor's rights would be defeated if the property could not be seized before judgment. Other states, mainly in New England, allow its use as a matter of right, and almost all law suits are commenced by an attachment procedure in those states.

Discussion of the particular grounds for attachment will be set forth subsequently, but in general, most states require an element of fraud, concealment, or removal from the jurisdiction before the remedy can be invoked.

The Federal Rules of Civil Procedure allow the seizure of property in Federal cases in accordance with the laws of the state in which the district court is held.

Exemptions

Every state has enacted exemption statutes which, to some extent, protect a debtor in the event his wages or property are subjected to legal process. These exemption statutes must be considered in dealing with attachments and garnishments.

Basically, an exemption statute sets off certain property of the debtor, leaving it free from any claims of creditors. Such statutes are meant to leave the debtor with a portion of his wages or property sufficient, in theory, to sustain himself and his family without relying upon public assistance.

The Consumer Credit Protection Act provides a basic wage exemption as against garnishments. Various state statutes likewise provide wage exemptions, some more restrictive than the Federal statute.

Most states provide an exemption known as a "homestead" exemption which protects a homeowner's principal place of residence from judicial process to an extent specified in the particular statute either in terms of dollar value or area.

All states extend to debtors an exemption of personal property, usually to be selected by the debtor from his household furnishings and fixtures. Some states specifically enumerate the household items which are to be held exempt, such as kitchen utensils and the like. Again, the purpose is to save the debtor from total destitution and allow him to continue, at least, a minimal way of life.

These then are the basic legal and economic aspects of garnishments and attachments. Exemptions are an inexorable part of these legal processes and must be considered when discussing the particular elements and ramifications of both legal processes.

Chapter Two

GARNISHMENTS

Garnishment of Wages before Judgment

Garnishment procedures and practices have traditionally been regulated by the states without Federal legislative or judicial intervention, and consequently have varied from jurisdiction to jurisdiction. Some states, such as Wisconsin, allowed the garnishment of wages or other personal earnings or compensation even prior to the creditor obtaining a judgment against the debtor in the principal action and without a determination of the merits of the claim.

The constitutionality of prejudgment garnishments, because of their obvious unjust results, has become the object of judicial interpretation; and, in fact, the Supreme Court of the United States has considered the question in the case of Sniadach v. Family Finance, 395 U.S. 337 (1969).

The Sniadach case arose in the State of Wisconsin. The Wisconsin statute on prejudgment garnishments provided that a plaintiff creditor seeking to invoke the prejudgment garnishment procedure against a debtor had to serve a summons and complaint on the debtor within ten days after service had been had on the person holding wages of the debtor.

Effectively, then, prejudgment garnishments could be had without notice being given to the debtor or without hearing at which he could voice his objections to the garnishment.

It is important to remember that the Supreme Court was not considering the question of prejudgment attachment of property, but rather the precise question of garnishment of personal wages prior to judgment against the debtor.

The Sniadach case was apparently one of those where principle outweighed economic considerations as the creditor's total claim, which arose out of a promissory note, amounted to $420. Wisconsin law exempted from garnishment fifty per cent of the employee's wages and in this case, $31.95 was to be withheld by the garnishee from the debtor's wages according to court order.

Although the debtor raised the question of the constitutionality of the prejudgment statute in the state courts, it was an unsuccessful attempt. These courts held that the temporary holding of the debtor's wages pending the final determination of the creditor's claim was not a deprivation of property without due process of law and not in violation of the Constitution. The Supreme Court found otherwise.

Justice Douglas, in writing the majority opinion for the Supreme Court, relied primarily on two theories. First, Justice Douglas reasoned that there was an absence of "extraordinary circumstances" which would justify the garnishment of wages prior to judgment without opportunity of hearing or notice to the debtor. By such reasoning, the Court elected not to disturb prior Supreme Court rulings which had sustained the constitutionality of prejudgment attachments when the circumstances warranted the invocation of such an extraordinary remedy.

Secondly, Justice Douglas reasoned that the case of wage garnishment is substantially different from the taking of other personal or real property.

> . "We deal here with wages--a specialized type of property presenting distinct problems in our economic system." Sniadach, page 340.

As was the rationale for the garnishment exemption portions of the Consumer Credit Protection Act, discussed previously, the taking of wages to the point where debtors were left destitute was the paramount reason for the Supreme Court's decision in the Sniadach case.

The Court did not, however, render all garnishments or attachments offensive, but rather only those which took employee's earnings without an opportunity of hearing or notice before final judgment had been rendered.

Since the Consumer Credit Protection Act does not prohibit the prejudgment garnishment of wages, and since the Sniadach case was concerned mainly with notice and hearing requirements, prejudgment garnishments can still be viable. It is possible that states will devise procedures whereby the debtor will be notified and given an opportunity to object to the garnishment procedure before it is finalized. A preliminary hearing might be the answer.

Of course, a preliminary hearing cannot be expected to elicit a final determination of the validity of the creditor's claim, but a creditor should at least be expected to establish probable cause for the need for the garnishment and prima facie evidence of the validity of his claims.

While prejudgment garnishments still exist in any manner, shape, or form, adequate safeguards should be installed so as to preclude fraudulent and unwarranted claims. Preliminary hearings, as may be suggested, probably would not be an effective means of protecting a debtor as most persons garnished cannot, or do not retain attorneys to represent them and their default or failure to appear at the hearing will result in the garnishment being completed.

The procedural requirements the Supreme Court would find acceptable for prejudgment garnishments are not crystal clear; but Justice Harlan, in his concurring opinion in the Sniadach case, specifically stated that due process of law was not satisfied by the Court's notification to the debtor of the garnishment, simultaneously with notice to the garnishee. Kentucky, for example, allows prejudgment garnishments if the creditor makes a written demand upon the debtor which notice advises the debtor of the grounds of suit and the right to a hearing. This procedure would presumably satisfy the tests established by the Supreme Court but cannot effectively eliminate the harsh results of prejudgment garnishment of wages.

Justice Harlan further objected to the theory that a prejudgment garnishment is only a temporary taking of property. Courts in various states had held that a prejudgment garnishment was not a violation of the due process provision of the Fourteenth Amendment as the property was only temporarily detained. If the judgment was later rendered in favor of the creditor, it was reasoned that the final deprivation of the debtor's property was the result of the final judgment and not the prejudgment garnishment.

Justice Black dissented in the Sniadach decision, not because he entirely disagreed with the majority as to the spirit of the decision, but rather because he felt it was the state legislature's prerogative to decide the relative merits of garnishment legislation. Justice Black believed that emotional rhetoric, proper in the legislative process, but having no place in judicial determinations, guided the majority in their decisions. The majority was unduly concerned with the fate of garnished debtors.

What, then, is the answer to prejudgment garnishment procedures? The Uniform Consumer Credit Code, approved by the American Bar Association, unequivocally recommends that prejudgment garnishments of wages, personal earnings or other compensation be abolished as they pertain to debts arising from consumer credit sales, consumer leases or consumer loans. The Code leaves open for debate the question of prejudgment garnishments when the creditor's claim arises from tortious (wrongful) conduct; but, of course, the scope of the Code extends only to consumer credit transactions.

Most states allow garnishment of accrued wages only after judgment has been obtained against the debtor; thus these states need not worry about complying with the nebulous ground rules established in the Sniadach case. Those states which must now comply can, as mentioned above, effectively circumvent the ruling by requiring preliminary hearings which most likely will be overlooked by the average debtor, to his peril.

The only answer, then, is complete abolishment of prejudgment garnishments. Why the Consumer Credit Protection Act did not deal with this particular problem is anybody's guess, so each state must recognize the harshness of this procedure and effectively deal with it.

Wisconsin and California have already recognized the errors of their ways and in 1969 enacted legislation expressly forbidding any garnishment of personal earnings of the principal defendant prior to judgment in the principal action. Other states including Arizona, Nevada and North Dakota must follow suit.

Garnishment of Wages after Judgment

Prior to Federal Legislation

Garnishment provisions of the Consumer Credit Protection Act became effective July 1, 1970, one year after the remaining provisions of the Act became effective. States, therefore, had a full year to conform their garnishment provisions to the Federal regulation after it was passed and two years from the time the legislation was introduced.

Many states did no have specific wage garnishment statutes, but rather applied their general attachment provisions to wage attachments. Even though the process is not called garnishment in several states, the process exists in almost every state in one form or another. Pennsylvania calls the process "judgment execution," while Montana, New Hampshire, Maine, and Vermont use the term "trustee process."

No matter the name given to the process, the end result is the same. Subsequent to judgment, a creditor can initiate, through the appropriate court, a process which results in an order upon the debtor's employer to withhold a specified portion of the debtor's wages.

While the Federal statute now sets a minimum exemption of wages from garnishment, there was and still is a tremendous divergence in the amount of exempted wages among the states. Some states such as Ohio differentiated between those persons who had head-of-the-household responsibilities and those who were single with no such responsibilities. Logically, the head of a household is and should be entitled to a larger exemption. Many states have continued this differentiation.

One hundred per cent exemptions are granted in Arkansas, California, Minnesota, Montana, Nevada, North Carolina, Pennsylvania, South Dakota, and Texas. Arizona allows a fifty per cent exemption. These and other states which allow a greater exemption than required by the Federal legislation, of course, did not have to revamp that provision of their respective statutes.

Another divergence pertaining to exempted wages concerns what a debtor must do to take advantage of the exemption. Some states, Idaho, Iowa, Kansas, and Nevada, required the debtor to file an affidavit claiming his statutory exemption. It is unlikely that many debtors were well enough educated in that area to take advantage of their legal rights. Since the Federal rule is mandatory as to exempted wages, this problem is now effectively eliminated.

Beyond the question of how much a creditor can take from a debtor's wages, lies the larger question of what result a garnishment could have on the debtor's employment. It is in this area that the Federal law has had the greatest effect. Employers who operated within the provisions of union contracts often negotiated a clause which would allow an employee to be discharged after being garnished a specified number of times within a specified period. Those employers who had no union contract or whose contract contained no such provision were at liberty to establish their own rules and regulations respecting garnishments.

Obviously an employer does not want to be burdened with the additional record keeping, accounting and judicial obligations which are imposed when an employee is garnished. An employer appears justified in being disgruntled at an employee who cannot conduct his own personal economic life so as not to interfere with his employment. Certainly an employer does not wish to be pestered by creditors who threaten to garnish employees' wages and an employer cannot help but question the integrity and ability of an employee who has economic problems to the extent of having his wages garnished with some frequency.

Prior to Federal legislation, an employer, not bound by contractual limitations, could discharge an employee upon being notified of an impending wage garnishment. An employee discharged on this ground had little recourse unless it could be shown that the employer somehow violated the employee's rights under the Federal labor laws. Numerous such cases have been heard by the National Labor Relations Board, with most cases being resolved in favor of the employer.

In the case of Michigan Lumber Fabricators, Inc., 111 NLRB 579 (1955), the Board held that the employer was justified in discharging the vice president of the union who had been served with his sixth garnishment notice. The gist of this case was an unfounded contention that the discharge was not for reason of the garnishments but rather discrimination against a high ranking union official.

Like the Michigan Lumber Fabricators, Inc. case, most of the reported National Labor Relations Board cases revolve around the question of whether the discharge was an attempt to discriminate against pro-union employees or truly based on excessive garnishments.

The Capital Electric Power Association was found to have violated the Labor Relations Act by discharging an employee on the charge of excessive garnishments when the Board determined that the real reason for the discharge was union activity. Evidence adduced at the hearing established that other employees although garnished with the same or greater frequency as the discharged employee, had not been discharged. Further, the employer had, in fact, aided other employees who had garnishment problems and the discharged employee had had no notice of such being the reason for his discharge. Capital Electric Power Assn., 171 NLRB No. 42 (1968).

The National Labor Relations Board likewise found a violation in the case of Campbell Tool Co., 112 NLRB 941 (1955). In that case the employee had been receiving garnishments for about one year prior to the discharge and only a small amount of the debt remained. Again, however, these were only factors tending to establish a discriminatory firing rather than an indictment of garnishments in general as a reason for discharge.

On the other hand, the National Labor Relations Board General Counsel in an Administrative Ruling (1959 F-915), held that an employer was completely justified in discharging an employee whose creditors were frequently annoying the employer with threatened garnishments so long as there was no evidence of any company hostility to the employee's exercise of his self-organizational rights.

A company's policy of discharging employees for excessive garnishments was approved by the United States Circuit Court of Appeals for the Fifth District in NLRB v. Georgia Rug Mill, 51 LRRM 2144 (1962); and a policy of discharge after two garnishments was okayed by the National Labor Relations Board in Federal Tool Corp., 130 NLRB 210 (1961).

It should now be readily apparent that employee discharges based on wage garnishments were not uncommon and not contrary to law as long as the discharge was truly for that reason and not an attempt to discriminate for union activities. It should also be apparent that an employer may well feel justified in discharging such employees, although many employees or unions have contended that discharge for garnishment is unduly harsh, unfair and medieval. An argument has been advanced that an employee s personal financial difficulties have no substantial relation to his employment and therefore should not be the basis for disciplinary action.

Perhaps, however, the most realistic justification for an employer's right to discharge can be found in the generally accepted theory of inherent management rights. That is, all rights not specifically prohibited or modified by collective bargaining agreements are reserved to management.

Prior to Federal legislation limiting management's inherent right, employer's subject only to limitations explained above could exercise their rights of discharging employees whose wages had been garnished.

Subsequent to Federal Legislation

The garnishment provisions of the Consumer Credit Protection Act became effective July 1, 1970, and in the interim period between its enactment and its effective date, many states revamped their garnishment statutes so as to comply with the Federal statute. Basically, the Federal legislation had the effect of increasing the amount of exempted wages in approximately 23 states and, of course, added the provision that an employee could not be discharged from his employment by reason of his being garnished for any one indebtedness. The Federal statute also provides that an employer who violates the garnishment provisions of the Act is subject to penalty.

Perhaps the most important result of the Federal legislation is not the provisions contained therein, but the effect that that statute has had on state statutes and the impetus it has provided for the adoption of uniform garnishment provisions throughout the United States.

The Act as it is set forth in Appendix A provides in substance that an employee's wages may be garnished in an amount not to exceed the lesser of twenty-five per cent of the employee's disposable earnings for any one week or the excess of weekly wages over an amount equal to thirty times the Federal minimum hourly wage.

Before examining exactly what this exemption means, it is important to note that every employer, no matter his involvement in interstate commerce, is covered by the scope of this particular Federal legislation. Even though this Act comes within those statutes classified as pertaining to commerce and trade, the reasons for the garnishment provisions in this Consumer Credit Protection Act cover commerce situations and go beyond the regulation of commerce and trade.

Congress has specifically set forth its findings and declaration of the purpose of the Act. Basically, Congress found that unrestricted garnishments of employees' wages could divert money into excessive credit payments and thereby hinder the production and flow of goods in interstate commerce, and at the same time, result in a loss of employment of the debtor which could disrupt production and consumption of goods. Either of these results could cause substantial burden on interstate commerce.

Beyond these findings affecting commerce, the great divergence among the states' statutes pertaining to garnishments has, in the thinking of Congress, destroyed much of the uniformity of the bankruptcy laws. The Federal government, of course, has the sole responsibility and control over the bankruptcy laws. Thus Congress has two justifications for imposing these garnishment laws on the states. There seems to be little question, however, that some day the Supreme Court will be asked to rule on whether or not the Federal government can affect this area which traditionally has been regulated by the states.

Definitions

The Federal statute employs the word "earnings" instead of "wages" in setting forth the amount of exemption. The statute itself defines earnings as "compensation paid or payable for personal services, whether denominated as wages, salary, commission, bonus or otherwise, and includes periodic payments pursuant to pension or retirement program."

Various statutes throughout the states employ such words as "wages," or "salary," or "earnings." When these words are used and not defined, a serious question arises as to what is covered in the term used. Earnings, of course, is a broader term than wages or salary as it may include income or earnings from a business in which the debtor is participating. For example, an attorney who has earnings but yet is not doing physical labor so as to earn wages or is not doing work to earn a salary is entitled to an exemption under a statute allowing exemption of earnings. Generally speaking, the exemption statutes passed by the several states did not provide for an exemption on commissions earned by an employee as does the Federal law. The Federal statute, then, is broader and all-inclusive and seems to cover any earnings due to an employee no matter how it is denominated.

Since the Federal legislation provides that the more restrictive of the state or Federal legislations shall apply, it appears that there will be considerable litigation as to the meaning of terms in the respective statutes. For example, Ohio provides that a garnishment pertains to "personal earnings." Does personal earnings in the Ohio statute have the same breadth of definition as earnings in the Federal statute?

The Federal legislation provides, as set forth above, that a certain percentage of disposable earnings are to be held as exempt from garnishment. The question then arises, "What is meant by disposable earnings?" Again, the statute sets forth a definition which says in substance that disposable earnings are those earnings which remian to the employee after deduction of any amounts required to be withheld by law.

This, of course, would include withholding tax and social security payments. It is assumed further that any deductions required for state or local income taxes would be such deductions but that union dues or initiation fees which are required to be deducted by reason of a contract between an employer and the union would not be used in the computation of disposable earnings. The administrator has also stated that unemployment compensation and workmen's compensation deductions when required by state law, are to be used in computing disposable earnings, but that an employee's share of health and welfare payments or credit union loan deductions are not.

Some authorities have suggested, however, that deductions to determine disposable earnings should include such items or medical and hospital insurance premiums deducted from an employee's pay.

The disposable earnings provision constitutes a substantial change in that most exemptions prior to the Federal legislation were computed upon gross earnings.

It is also interesting to note that the Federal legislation makes no differentiation between employees who are charged with the responsibility of supporting a household as opposed to those who are single and have no responsibilities other than to themselves. Many of the state laws prior to the Federal enactment differentiated between the head of a household and single persons in the amount of exempted wages.

Ohio, for exampke, provided that if the employee was the chief support of a family or was paying alimony, maintenance or other allowance for the support of a divorced or separated spouse or was responsible for the support of a minor child or even the chief support of any dependent person or was a widow, the amount of exempted wages was significantly higher than if such employee was not any of those enumerated persons.

The reason, of course, for the differentiation between classifications of persons was that a person charged with responsibility of providing for others needs more in the way of exempted wages to meet those responsibilities than a single person or person not having such responsibilities. It would appear that this is a valid classification and probably should have in some way been adopted by the Federal legislation.

If the particular state law does make a responsibility classification and provides for a greater exemption for persons having such responsibilities in excess of the minimum exemption provided by the Federal statute, then the state statute will still be viable and such person will presumably be granted the greater exemption.

The Consumer Credit Protection Act also defines the term "garnishment." For purpose of application of the Federal legislation, garnishment is any proceeding whether it be equitable or legal through which the earnings of an employee are required to be withheld for payment of a debt.

The reason why this definition was included in the statute is that many states, as previously mentioned, do not refer to the process as garnishment as such, and garnishment can also mean an execution upon property other than personal earnings. The Federal legislation then is specific as to the scope of its application.

The term "individual" is used in the Act as opposed to "employee" or "wage earner, laborer, or mechanic." The use of this term amounts to a broadening of the persons covered and also eliminates definitional problems such as who is an employee or what functions constitute the class of laborer or mechanic.

Once the definitional problems have been overcome, the problem of how often and when garnishments can be instituted becomes important to consider.

Pay Periods

The Federal legislation makes no mention of the number of times an employee may be garnished in any one month or any specific time period and bases its computation of the exemption on weekly wages. It does not define or set a garnishment period. Some states, such as Ohio and Delaware, provide that a successful garnishment may be brought only once during any thirty-day period. This, of course, limits the number of successful garnishments that can be had against any one employee, while the Federal legislation seems to permit garnishments as frequently as one per week. It is important, then, to check the particular state statute to determine frequency in which garnishments can be granted. The computation of exempted earnings based on weekly, bi-weekly, or monthly payrolls may vary from state to state, but the end result must not be an exemption less than provided by the Federal statute.

As mentioned previously, a significant factor arising from the Federal legislation has been the proposal of uniform state legislation. The Uniform Consumer Credit Code was drafted by the Conference of Commissioners on Uniform State Law and approved by the American Bar Association. Unlike the Consumer Credit Protection Act, the Uniform Code takes into account pay periods other than weekly and sets a higher minimum on the exemption of wages. In those states which adopt the Code, the maximum of wages that can be garnished would be the lesser of twenty-five per cent of disposable earnings (disposable earnings having the same definition as employed under Federal statute), for a week or an amount of disposable earnings which exceeds forty times the Federal minimum hourly wage. This represents an increase of ten times the Federal minimum hourly wage over what is provided in the Consumer Credit Protection Act. The Uniform Code further provides that if the pay period is other than weekly, the exemption is to be based on forty times the Federal minimum hourly wage for the monthly, bi-monthly, or other pay period basis.

The Secretary of Labor through the Administrator of the Wage and Hour Division, is vested with the responsibility of providing by regulation a multiple of the Federal minimum wage equivalent in the case of pay periods other than a week. The regulations have established that the number of work weeks or fractions thereof times thirty times the applicable Federal minimum wage shall be used as the formula in computing allowable garnishments. A calendar month is considered to be 4-1/3 work weeks.

Accordingly, a $96 exemption would be allowed for an employee paid every two weeks. In applying the formula, one would multiply 2, the number of work weeks, by 30 by $1.60, the current Federal minimum wage, to arrive at $96 as the exemption.

If an employee is paid monthly, one would multiply 4-1/3 weeks by 30 by $1.60 and arrive at $208 as the exemtpion.

If an employee is paid semi-monthly, one would multiply 2-1/6 by 30 by $1.60 to arrive at an exemption of $104.

Once the applicable amounts of wages which can be taken and the exemption which must be granted have been determined, these figures must be, so to speak, plugged into the appropriate state procedural statutes, which are the next consideration.

Chart I lists the exemption afforded state-by-state.

CHART I

PRIMARY FEATURES OF STATE EXEMPTION STATUTES

State	Exemption (or maximum amount subject to garnishment)
ALABAMA	Exemption, 75% of wages, salaries or other compensation of laborers or employees.
ALASKA	Head of Household--$350 due or received in 30-day period--if needed for support.
ARIZONA	Exemption, 50% of earnings for 30 days before service of garnishment--if necessary for support.
ARKANSAS	Claimed exemption for laborers and mechanics, 60 days of earnings up to $200 for single person and $500 for head of household.
	Automatic exemption--first $25 of net wages.
CALIFORNIA	Exemption, 100% of earnings of head of household.

CHART I (continued)

State	Exemption (or maximum amount subject to garnishment)
COLORADO	Head of Household -- 70% of earnings exempt.
CONNECTICUT	Exemption, the greater of 75% of disposable earnings or $65, or 40 times Federal minimum hourly wage.
DELAWARE	Exemptions vary from county to county. New Castle County, 90% exemption on debts for necessaries or state taxes.
DISTRICT OF COLUMBIA	Wages: Garnishment cannot exceed 10% of first $200 of gross wages; 20% of $200-$500 gross wages; 50% of excess--calendar month.
	Other Earnings: Exemption -- $200 of earnings for 2-month period for resident and head of household based on combined husband and wife earnings.
	Single person--first $60 of earnings for 2-month period exempt.
FLORIDA	100% exemption--head of household.
GEORGIA	Exemption, the greater of 75% of disposable earnings or 30 times Federal minimum hourly wage.
HAWAII	Exemption, 95% of first $100 per month; 90% of next $100; 80% of excess.
IDAHO	Maximum garnishment -- the lesser of 25% of disposable earnings or excess of 30 times Federal minimum hourly wage.

CHART I (continued)

State	Exemption (or maximum amount subject to garnishment)
ILLINOIS	Exemption: The greater of: Head of household--$65 per week; single person--$50 per week; or 85% of earnings, not to exceed $200 per week.
INDIANA	Head of Household--$15 a week and 90% of excess exempt.
IOWA	All persons--maximum garnishment by any one creditor, $150 plus costs.
KANSAS	Exemption, the greater of 75% of disposable earnings or 30 times the Federal minimum hourly wage.
KENTUCKY	Exemption, the greater of 75% of disposable earnings or 30 times the Federal minimum hourly wage.
LOUISIANA	Exemption, the greater of 75% of disposable earnings or 30 times the Federal minimum hourly wage, but not less than $70 a week of disposable earnings.
MAINE	$40 of wages due and payable, $10 in any case exempt.
MARYLAND	Exemption, the greater of $100 times number of week's wages or 75% of same.
	Specific Counties: Greater of 75% of wages due or 30 times Federal minimum hourly wage are exempt.

CHART I (continued)

State	Exemption (or maximum amount subject to garnishment)
MASSACHUSETTS	Exemption, $80 of wages per week, $40 per week of pension.
MICHIGAN	First Garnishment: Exemption, Head of Household--60% of wages, maximum, $50; minimum, $30 for week. Pay period in excess of week, maximum, $90; minimum, $60. Exemption, Others--40% of wages, minimum, $20; maximum, $50. Subsequent Garnishments--Exemption Head of Household--60% of wages, maximum, $30; minimum, $12 for week. Pay period over 16 days, maximum, $60; minimum, $30. Others--30% of wages, maximum, $20; minimum, $10.
MINNESOTA	Maximum Garnishment--Lesser of 25% of disposable earnings, or excess of 8 times number of business days and paid holidays (not exceeding 5 in any week) times the Federal minimum hourly wage. 100% exemption if earnings needed for family support.
MISSISSIPPI	75% of earnings for residents are exempt.
MISSOURI	Head of Household--90% of wages for 30-day period are exempt.

CHART I (continued)

State	Exemption (or maximum amount subject to garnishment)
MONTANA	Head of Household--100% of exemption for 45-day period before garnishment, but if debt is for necessaries or gasoline, 50% exempt.
NEBRASKA	Head of Household--85% of wages exempt.
NEVADA	Maximum Garnishment--Lesser of 25% of disposable earnings or excess over 30 times Federal minimum hourly wage.
NEW HAMPSHIRE	Exemption, 100% of wages earned after service of garnishment. 100% of wages earned before service unless judgment rendered by a New Hampshire Court, then 50 times Federal minimum hourly wage per week. 100%--earnings of wife and children exempt.
NEW JERSEY	Exemption, 10% of earnings over $48 per week. Court may increase percentage of garnishment on employee's earnings in excess of $25000 per year.
NEW MEXICO	Exemption, greater of 75% of disposable earnings of each pay or 40 times the Federal minimum hourly wage per week.
NEW YORK	Court of Record Exemption, 90% of income where employee earns at least $85 per week, 100% if employee earns less.

CHART I (continued)

State	Exemption (or maximum amount subject to garnishment)
NEW YORK (cont'd.)	Court Not of Record Exemption, 10% of earnings subject to garnishment of employee earning $30 or more per week if such employee resides or works in city of 250,000 or more; 10% of earnings of employees not meeting such residence or working locality test but earning $25 a week.
NORTH CAROLINA	Head of Household--100% of earnings for 60 days before service are exempt.
NORTH DAKOTA	Head of Household--Resident: $50 per week plus $5 for each dependent up to $25 are exempt. Non-Resident Head of Household: $35 per week is exempt.
OHIO	Exemption, greater of 82.5% of disposable earnings for 30-day period, or 175 times Federal minimum hourly wage.
OKLAHOMA	Consumer Obligations--Garnishment can take lesser of 25% of disposable weekly earnings or excess of 30 times Federal minimum hourly wage. Other Obligations--100% exemption for 90-day period, resident head of household; 75% if wages not required for support of family.
OREGON	Maximum Garnishment--Lesser of 25% of disposable earnings for one week, or excess of 30 times Federal minimum hourly wage.

CHART I (continued)

State	Exemption (or maximum amount subject to garnishment)
PENNSYLVANIA	100% exemption except for 4 weeks board and lodging, support payments, taxes or alimony.
RHODE ISLAND	$50 per week exemption.
SOUTH CAROLINA	Head of Household--100% exemption except for obligations for necessaries for which 15% of wages up to $100 may be taken.
SOUTH DAKOTA	100% exemption for head of household.
TENNESSEE	Head of Household--Exemption greater of 50% of net weekly income, or $20; maximum, $50 per week.
TEXAS	100% exemption as per State Constitution.
UTAH	Head of Household or Married Men -- Minimum exemption $50, maximum 50% of earnings for 30-day period.
	Consumer transactions--Exemption equal to greater of 75% of disposable earnings or 40 times Federal minimum hourly wage.
VERMONT	Exemption, $30 of weekly wages plus 50% of wages in excess of $60.
VIRGINIA	Maximum garnishment, lesser of 25% of disposable earnings or excess of 30 times Federal minimum hourly wage.

CHART I (continued)

State	Exemption (or maximum amount subject to garnishment)
WASHINGTON	Exemption, greater of 75% of disposable earnings or 40 times state minimum wage.
WEST VIRGINIA	Exemption, 80% of earnings for persons earning over $20 per week.
WISCONSIN	Exemption, greater of 75% of disposable weekly earnings or 30 times Federal minimum hourly wage.
WYOMING	Exemption, head of household, 50% of earnings for 60-day period before service.

Proposed Uniform Consumer Credit Code:
Maximum garnishment, lesser of 25% of disposable earnings for one week or excess of 40 times Federal minimum hourly wage.

Consumer Credit Protection Act:
Maximum garnishment, 25% of weekly disposable earnings, or excess of 30 times Federal minimum hourly wage.

Procedure

The Federal legislation does not present specific guidelines for the initiation and follow-through of the garnishment procedure. Neither does the proposed Uniform Consumer Credit Code. State statutes, such as Ohio, do provide specific procedures to be followed. For example, under the Ohio statute which became effective on September 16, 1970, a person seeking to attach the personal earnings of a debtor must make a demand in writing for the amount of the obligation due over and above the exempt portion of the debtor's wages. That notice must contain information stating the name of the creditor, the date on which the judgment was taken against the debtor and notice that if the debt is not paid within the fifteen days of the date of the mailing of the notice, that the garnishment procedure through the court will be initiated.

The notice prescribed by the Ohio statute gives the debtor an option of either paying the full amount due, paying the nonexempt portion of his wages directly to the creditor, or applying to the local municipal or county court for the appointment of a trustee who will apportion his earnings among various creditors. The notice contains specifications establishing the amount of wages that the debtor is responsible to the creditor for over and above the amount of exempted wages. The creditor must send this demand to the debtor at least fifteen days and not more than forty-five days before he seeks an order of garnishment through the appropriate court.

If the debtor does not respond to the demand notice, the creditor may commence the garnishment proceedings by filing an affidavit stating the name of the defendant, the name of the person, partnership, or corporation who is holding funds representing personal wages due to the debtor, an affirmation that demand has been sent to the debtor as required by law, that payment as requested by the demand notice has not been paid and that the creditor, or attorney, or agent making the affidavit has no knowledge of the debtor making application or having had the appointment of a trustee so as to preclude the garnishment of his personal earnings.

The creditor must file along with the affidavit and the specifications above set forth, the return receipt or other proof of service on the debtor of the demand.

After these documents have been filed with the court, the court is to submit to the garnishee, the employer holding personal wages of the debtor, three copies of the garnishment order. The garnishee then has the responsibility of filing one copy with the court, keeping one for his records, and delivering one to the employee at the time he would normally pay him. The garnishee is responsible for all funds owed to the employee at the time he is served with the written notice. As previously stated, in Ohio an employee can only be garnished successfully once within any thirty-day period and the amount of exposure is the lesser of $17-1/2$ per cent of the monthly wages after deductions required by law or the excess of monthly wages after required deductions over an amount equal to 175 times the current Federal minimum hourly wage.

The garnishee is required by law to comply with the order of court and his failure to do so can result in contempt of court proceedings or liability for the amount due under the order.

After the garnishee has been served with written notice, he is required, under the Ohio statutes, to appear and answer within the specified time. He must, under oath, answer all questions put to him concerning the property or wages that he holds for the benefit of the debtor. The garnishee is then responsible for paying the amount owed by him concerning the property or wages that he holds for the benefit of the debtor. The garnishee upon paying the funds, is discharged from liability to the debtor for the money so paid into court and is not subject to costs beyond those caused by his own resistance to the claims against him.

Discharge from Employment

Perhaps the most significant change which the Federal legislation brought about was the provision prohibiting an employer from discharging an employee by reason of the fact that he has been garnished on any one indebtedness. Since the Federal legislation does not specify that this garnishment must pertain to a debt which has arisen by reason of consumer purchases, loans, or other consumer transactions as have been specified in the proposed Uniform Consumer Credit Code, it may be assumed that the garnishment can pertain to debts arising from tortious conduct, breach of contract, etc. However, the Federal legislation is explicit in prohibiting an employer from discharging an employee because of the fact that his earnings have been subjected to a garnishment for any one indebtedness. This leaves open the possibility that an employee may still be discharged if he receives a garnishment upon a second indebtedness be it contract, consumer credit transaction or tortious conduct. It is reasonable to assume that an employee who receives a garnishment because of one indebtedness is in such dire financial condition that he will be subjected to subsequent garnishments on other indebtednesses and that the Federal legislation will have no redeeming value to him in so far as protecting his employment. It is, however, a step in the right direction.

Some states, such as Ohio, provide similar restrictions against the employer. Ohio, for example, provides that an employer cannot discharge an employee because his earnings have been subjected to garnishment once in any twelve-month period. This particular provision of the Ohio statute seems to be less restrictive than the Federal legislation and would appear that the Federal legislation would take precedence in determining whether or not an employer has a right to discharge an employee.

In examining the Consumer Credit Protection Act with respect to discharged employees for reasons of garnishment, several questions immediately appear. For instance, what is meant by one indebtedness? Can an employer discipline an employee short of discharging him for the reason that his wages have been garnished?

In response to questions posed to the Administrator of the Wage and Hour Division of the Department of Labor, he has offered an opinion on these problems. One indebtedness is taken to mean a single garnishment procedure. In other words, a single garnishment procedure can be initiated with garnishments occurring as frequently as one per week and it is possible that creditors may join together in that garnishment procedure and continue it until all of their claims have been satisfied. So long as a second garnishment procedure is not initiated, an employee is safe from discharge under the Consumer Credit Protection Act.

Many union contracts or employer's rules provide a warning system whereby an employee is given official notice of a warning and upon receiving a specified number of warnings, may be discharged. Since the Consumer Credit Protection Act only says that an employee may not be discharged by reason of a garnishment on any one indebtedness, it leaves open the possibility of warnings and other disciplinary action against him by reason of the garnishment.

The Administrator has, on this question, also rendered an opinion. In his opinion, a warning given to an employee, which warning counts towards the number required for his discharge, is a violation of the Act. Although warnings per se are not violative of the Act, a subsequent discharge which in effect is a result of warnings for garnishments would be violative in that the subsequent discharge really would be for the reason that the employee's wages were garnished.

It is not clear whether an employer can suspend an employee for repeated garnishments on any one indebtedness without being in violation of the Act. The reason for this indefinite opinion is that the suspension could very well result in an effective or constructive discharge of the employee. Upon being suspended, the employee might seek employment elsewhere and in effect then, the suspension as a result of the repeated garnishments on the one indebtedness might be tantamount to the firing or discharge. It would appear that each particular case would have to be determined on its merits to reach a conclusion as to the effect of the suspension and its connection with garnishment on any one indebtedness.

A further question which at this time is not answered is whether or not a debtor who incurs another debt with the same creditor who has initiated garnishment proceedings or increases his debt by means of a further purchase on an open account, the normal charge account situation, is entitled to employment protection if the creditor initiates a subsequent garnishment proceeding on the enlarged or subsequent debt. The question turns upon the point of whether or not this enlargement or subsequent debt to the same creditor would result in a garnishment on an indebtedness different from the original one. If it is determined that this is a second indebtedness, then the employee is not entitled to further protection under the Act, but if it is determined that this is truly an extension of the first indebtedness, then of course, he cannot be discharged.

Even though the Act provides that an employee may not be discharged by reason of a single indebtedness, he may be afforded protection under the Act on a subsequent garnishment. This situation might arise where there is a considerable lapse of time between the garnishments so as to eliminate the first indebtedness as a material consideration, but it would appear that there must be a considerable time differential.

Several states have taken the initiative in providing their own employee protection provisions.

California provides that an employee cannot be discharged by reason of a garnishment for any one indebtedness prior to final order or judgment of court. Connecticut provides that an employee cannot be disciplined, suspended or discharged unless he has received more than seven garnishments in any calendar year.

Delaware provides that it is unlawful for an employer to dismiss an employee for garnishment. No limitation as to time or number of garnishments is included in the Act.

Georgia basically follows the Federal act, providing that the employer cannot discharge an employee for garnishment for any one indebtedness but adds the stipulation that the garnishment may be for state taxes.

Hawaii provides that an employee can't be suspended or discharged because he was garnished or because he has filed a petition under the wage earner plan of the Bankruptcy Act.

Kansas provides that an employer cannot discharge an employee by reason of garnishment on any one indebtedness.

Kentucky also follows the Federal act.

The statutes of Maryland provide that an employer cannot discharge an employee by reason of an employee's wages being garnished on any one occasion in any calendar year.

Michigan law provides that no employer can discharge an employee solely by reason of garnishment.

Minnesota provides that an employer cannot discharge an employee for reason of garnishment unless the employee has been garnished more than three times within ninety days on more than one indebtedness.

Montana provides that an employee cannot be discharged or laid off by reason of a garnishment served on his employer.

The state of New York provides that no employee can be discharged or laid off by reason of the fact that he has been garnished.

Ohio provides that an employee cannot be discharged solely for the reason of garnishment if he receives no more than one garnishment in any twelve-month period.

The Vermont statutes provide that it is unlawful for an employer to discharge an employee simply because an employee has been garnished. But, if an employee has been garnished on five or more separate occasions which garnishees have arisen from separate actions, the employee may be discharged.

Virginia law provides that an employee cannot be discharged for garnishment for any indebtedness.

Washington provides that an employee can be discharged by reason of garnishment if he has been garnished on three or more indebtednesses within twelve consecutive months.

Wisconsin, which as previously mentioned, initiated a number of new provisions pertaining to garnishment, states that an employee cannot be discharged by reason of the fact that his earnings have been garnished for any one indebtedness.

The Consumer Credit Protection Act provides a penalty against an employer who violates the Act with respect to discharge of an employee. A willful violation of this provision carries with it a criminal prosecution and a fine of up to $1,000 or imprisonment for not more than one year or both.

The proposed Uniform Commercial Credit Code gives the discharged employee a civil cause of action against his employer. The employee may recover wages and seek an order of reinstatement to his employment. The employee's damages shall be equal to his lost wages but in no case shall exceed lost wages for six weeks.

The state of Minnesota has provided in its act that an employee has a right to bring a civil action if he does so within ninety days of the date of discharge. He may recover twice the amount of his wages lost as a result of the violation of the Minnesota statute.

Assignment of Wages

The Federal act specifically exempts from its application court orders for support, bankruptcy, or attempts to collect state or federal income taxes. The Administrator of the Wage and Hour Division of the Department of Labor has also expressed an opinion as to assignment of wages. In his opinion, an assignment of wages, which is a private contractual transaction by which the right to receive wages is transferred from an employee to a creditor, should not be within the scope and protection of the Federal act.

Most states now permit an employee to enter into such contracts for the assignment of wages, both already earned and to be earned in the future, and it is conceivable that this method of getting at an employee's wages might take on more significance in light of the more restrictive garnishment laws.

Few states have put a limit on the amount of wages which can be taken under assignment, but most require that the employer consent to, or at least be notified of the assignment. It is a common provision that the spouse of the employee making the assignment consent to it, and that the assignment must be in writing, signed by the employee. Certain states require the assignment to be recorded, and others require it to be executed with formalities usually reserved for deeds and mortgages.

Since it is possible that wage assignments might take on added significance as creditors grasp for more effective means to secure collection of consumer obligations, the primary provisions of each state's statute have been included herein and set forth in Chart II.

CHART II

WAGE ASSIGNMENTS

State

ALABAMA — Not permitted.

ALASKA — No provision.

ARIZONA — Assignment valid, payment for a loan:

1. Must be in writing.
2. Consent of spouse living with assignor must be given.
3. Assignment cannot exceed 10% of assignor's wages, salary or other compensation.
4. Assignment period cannot exceed 48 months.

ARKANSAS — Assignment must be consented to by wife in writing.

Assignment must be approved by employer and filed with county recorder.

CALIFORNIA — Permitted with qualification as to writing, consent of spouse or guardian.

CHART II (continued)

State

COLORADO — Assignment void as to small loans. All other void and unenforceable can be honored by employer if in writing, for a fixed period of not more than 30 days and a copy mailed to employer and employee.

CONNECTICUT — Not permitted.

DELAWARE — Not permitted, with exception as to certain real estate transactions.

DISTRICT OF COLUMBIA — Not permitted.

FLORIDA — Proceeds of loan must be paid to the borrower simultaneously with execution of assignment.

GEORGIA — No provision.

HAWAII — Valid if in writing, signed by borrower and spouse.

IDAHO — Valid up to 10% of debtor's earnings and if proceeds of loan paid to borrower simultaneously with execution of assignment.

ILLINOIS — Permitted with qualifications as to disclosure, type of obligation, and notice.

INDIANA — Permitted with qualifications as to notice, consent of spouse and period of earnings covered.

CHART II (continued)

State	
IOWA	Permitted up to 10% of debtor's wages and with qualification as to writing, notice, and consent of spouse.
KANSAS	Limited to 10% of wages or other earnings with qualification as to notice. Employer is given the option whether or not to honor the assignment.
KENTUCKY	Employer must consent; maximum assignment is 10% of wages owing.
LOUISIANA	Employer must consent; proceeds of loan must be paid simultaneously with execution of assignment.
MAINE	Employer must have actual notice; assignment must be recorded.
MARYLAND	Not permitted as to future wages; allowed as to earned wages with qualifications as to writing, notice and consent of spouse.
MASSACHUSETTS	Permitted with qualifications as to disclosures, writing, consent of spouse, and recording.
MICHIGAN	Limited to 10% of wages; copy must be served upon the employer.
MINNESOTA	Permitted with qualifications as to writing, notice and consent of employer.
MISSISSIPPI	Permitted if notice is given to employer before consummation of contract or delivery of goods, and employer accepts.

CHART II (continued)

State	
MISSOURI	Void as to future earnings; assignments of past earnings must be in writing and make certain disclosure.
MONTANA	Permitted with qualifications as to consent of spouse, notice to employer, recording and period of wages covered.
NEBRASKA	Permitted with qualifications as to consent by spouse.
NEVADA	Not permitted.
NEW HAMPSHIRE	Permitted if in writing and recorded.
NEW JERSEY	Permitted if consented to by spouse, in writing, and signed by borrower.
NEW MEXICO	Acceptable if consented to by spouse, recorded, and proceeds of loan delivered to debtor simultaneously with execution of assignment.
NEW YORK	Permitted on indebtedness of more than $1000 with qualifications as to type of instrument, disclosures, filing and limitations as to liability of guarantor and effectiveness.
NORTH DAKOTA	Void as to future earnings.
OHIO	Limited to 25% of earnings of married persons; and requires consent of spouse.
OKLAHOMA	Not permitted.

CHART II (continued)

State

OREGON	Limited to 10% of debtor's earnings; copy to be served upon employer.
PENNSYLVANIA	Permitted if in writing, accepted by the employer and consented to by spouse.
RHODE ISLAND	Permitted if in writing, delivered to employer, and making certain disclosures.
SOUTH CAROLINA	Employer must give written consent.
SOUTH DAKOTA	No provision.
TEXAS	Employer must be given written notice immediately after the debtor's execution of the assignment.
UTAH	Employee can authorize payroll deductions if the authorization is revokable. (It appears Utah has adopted at least in part, the Uniform Consumer Credit Code.)
VERMONT	Service must be had upon the employer.
VIRGINIA	Permitted if employer consents and proper disclosures are made.
WASHINGTON	Permitted with qualification as to amount of obligation, notice, recording and consent of spouse.
WEST VIRGINIA	Limited for period of one year, qualification as to writing and disclosures.
WISCONSIN	Permitted with qualifications as to consent of spouse and formalities of execution.

CHART II (continued)

State

WYOMING — Employer must accept, assignment must be recorded, spouse must consent.

State laws, too, exempt certain portions of wages which are subject to other claims or are peculiar in some other way from the general garnishment provisions. Representative of those types of exempted transactions are the following:

State	Exemption
Alaska	Child support payments either taken as an automatic payroll deduction or to be paid by court order.
Arkansas	Wages subject to garnishment are to exclude deductions required by law as well as group life, hospitalization and retirement payments.
Connecticut	Support payments for wife or minor children have first priority.
Georgia	Alimony payments ordered by the court are exempt.
Idaho	Bankruptcy orders, obligations due on state or federal taxes, and ordered support payments are exempt from general garnishment laws.
Iowa	Normal wage exemptions don't apply to claims for alimony and child support.

State	Exemption
Michigan	Wages subject to garnishment are to exclude sums due under order of court for alimony and support.
Nebraska	Exemptions normally granted are not available to employees who have left or are about to leave the state.
Nevada	General garnishment laws don't apply to court orders in bankruptcy or for support or to obligations due on state or federal taxes.
Oregon	General garnishment laws don't apply to court orders in bankruptcy or for support or to obligations due on state or federal taxes.
Tennessee	Exemptions normally extended don't apply to obligations for support of children or alimony orders.
Washington	Exemptions don't apply to orders for support rendered by the courts.

These provisions mean, generally, that either the garnishment laws do not apply at all, or the exemption normally extended to the debtor will not be considered when the garnishment has been initiated to collect one of the enumerated types of obligations.

The term "exemption" in context so far has meant that portion of wages which cannot be taken by garnishment or certain transactions which are exempt from application of the garnishment law. There is, however, a further use of the term "exemption" which becomes significant when comparing the application of state laws to that of the federal law.

State Exemptions from Federal Law

Rules and regulations promulgated by the Administrator of the Wage and Hour Division of the Department of Labor, who is charged with the responsibility of policing the garnishment provisions of the Consumer Credit Protection Act, set forth procedures which a state must follow in seeking an exemption of their laws from the Federal Act.

Each state seeking such exemption must file a request for exemption in duplicate with the Administrator. Notice of the filing is to be published in the Federal Register so as to allow interested persons an opportunity to make comments upon the application.

The Administrator has stated that the state laws should be scrutinized as to the persons protected and the type of transaction covered by each statute. Of course, the maximum allowable garnishment cannot be exceeded and an undue burden procedurally cannot be placed on the debtor. The latter provision presumably relates to state provisions which require a debtor to file an exemption claim.

Numerous states base exemptions on proof that the debtor's wages are needed for support of the family. Arkansas, for example, provides a basic automatic exemption, but also provides a 60-day wage exemtpion if the debtor files an affidavit stating that wages for the 60 days together with other personal property doesn't exceed the constitutional limit provided in that state. A provision such as that will not meet Federal approval for exemption purposes.

On information received from the Wage and Hour Division in December, 1970, the following states have filed exemption applications:

> Illinois
> Kansas
> Kentucky
> New Hampshire
> North Carolina
> Ohio
> South Carolina
> Virginia

As of December, 1970, only the State of Ohio which revised its garnishment statutes in September, 1970, presumably in an attempt to meet Federal restrictions, has been denied exemption. The remainder of the applications were still pending at that time.

The major problem under the Ohio statute is its interpretation. The statute provides that the maximum garnishment is to be the lesser of 17.5 per cent of monthly earnings after deductions required by law, or the excess of monthly earnings over an amount equal to 175 times the current Federal minimum hourly wage. Some courts have interpreted the 17.5 per cent limitation on monthly, or 30-day periods, to mean that if an employee is paid on a weekly basis that the creditor is entitled to 4 times 17.5 per cent, or 70 per cent of that week's pay. This obviously violates the Federal provision.

Other courts within the state and the state's Attorney General's office, have interpreted the 17.5 per cent provision to mean that there can be a maximum deduction of 17.5 per cent on one paycheck a month.

Since the Consumer Credit Protection Act does not limit the number of garnishments which can be filed, Ohio is considering removing its once-in-every-30-days limitation and allowing garnishment of each paycheck, weekly, bi-weekly, or semi-monthly. Creditors could then effectively take up to 75 per cent of a debtor's monthly wages. Obviously, both unions and employers are opposed to this type of arrangement as it would be costly to employers and detrimental to employees.

There appears little doubt that Ohio's statute must be revamped in several areas. The Administrator's opinion set forth hereafter gives rise to that inescapable conclusion. What appeared to the Ohio Legislature as an act in strict compliance with the Consumer Credit Protection Act turned out to be so indefinite in meaning and so vague in procedure that it must be amended or dropped entirely in favor of uniform state legislation.

On November 25, 1970, Robert D. Moran, Administrator of the Wage and Hour Division, United States Department of Labor, considered the matter of the state of Ohio's application for exemption under the Consumer Credit Protection Act. The basic test for exemption is whether or not the state statute is substantially similar to the provisions of the Federal legislation. Basically, Mr. Moran concluded that even though the Ohio garnishment provisions provided an employee a greater protection on a monthly basis, the provisions setting forth maximum limitations on garnishment were not substantially similar to the restrictions of the Federal legislation when employed on a weekly basis. Ohio, as mentioned previously, permits only one garnishment per month and limits said garnishment to 17.5 per cent of monthly earnings. This effectively can result in 70 per cent of weekly earnings being garnished. Since it has been determined by survey in the State of Ohio that the majority of employees had pay periods shorter than one month, the effective results of the application of the Ohio law would be substantially dissimilar and substantially less restrictive than the Federal legislation.

It was obviously the Ohio legislature's intention that its law, effective September 1970, be read in a manner not inconsistent with the provisions of the Consumer Credit Protection Act, but Mr. Moran concluded that the inconsistencies between the Act and the Ohio provisions as they affect employees having pay periods shorter than one month, could not be overcome and accordingly denied the State of Ohio's application for exemption.

Another provision of the Ohio law which made it substantially dissimilar to the Federal Act was that Ohio limited its exemption from garnishment to personal earnings for services rendered and therefore did not cover, in the Administrator's opinion, periodic payments under pension and retirement plans as well as bonuses and commissions which are covered by the Consumer Credit Protection Act.

The Administrator also raised the question of what protection the Ohio Act afforded non-residents, as no specific mention of non-residents was set forth in the statute and whether or not the exemption was automatic or had to be raised as an affirmative defense.

It is interesting to note that the Secretary of Labor filed suit against the Cleveland Municipal Court in order to obtain an interpretation of the Ohio statute. Upon recommendation of the Federal District Court, a meeting was held between the Wage and Hour Administrator and the attorneys from the Ohio Attorney General's Office. Close scrutinization was given to the Ohio law and it was determined that regardless of how often an employee is paid, his exemption is to be based on the aggregate of his disposable earnings for the previous 30-day period prior to the garnishment. Even though the Ohio law is explicit as to the procedural requirements and safeguards afforded an employee in that regard, the Administrator concluded that the only basis for comparison is the amount of the exemption from garnishment. It was concluded that since Ohio permits the deduction for garnishment of 17.5 per cent of monthly earnings from the last paycheck of the month and the law can be interpreted to mean that 70 per cent of the final paycheck may be garnished, it is less restrictive than the Federal legislation which protects 75 per cent of the weekly personal earnings of any employee.

The opinion of the Administrator points out that in a recent survey of large cities throughout the United States, the overwhelming majority of workers received wage payments for smaller than monthly pay periods. In Ohio cities more than 88 per cent of all plant workers received payment weekly and in some Ohio cities, the weekly pay rate is as high as 98 per cent. Office workers in the Ohio cities surveyed were found to be paid weekly, biweekly, or bi-monthly in greater percentage than those that are paid monthly. In view of the results of this survey, it was concluded that the Ohio law could not be substantially similar to the Federal legislation.

The Administrator set forth illustrations which were as follows:

WORKWEEK	OHIO EXEMPTION		SUBJECT TO
	82.5%	175 x $1.60	GARNISHMENT
1. $100	$330	$280	$70
2. $100	$330	$280	$70
3. $100	$330	$280	$70
4. $100	$330	$280	$70

It is obvious from this illustration that $70 can be withheld from the paycheck for the last workweek of the month. This would leave the employee with only $30 for that week. Effectively then, there would have been a 70 per cent garnishment of the disposable earnings for weekly workweek number 4.

The disparity even becomes greater when an employee, for instance, would earn $90 in the first workweek, $110 in the second, $100 in the third, and only $60 in the fourth. Under the Ohio exemption, he would be entitled to $297 if it is computed on the 82.5

per cent exemption and $280 if it is computed on the 175 times the Federal minimum hourly wage. The amount of his disposable earnings subject to garnishment for the month would be $63; that is, his total earnings of $360 less the exemption of $297. If the garnishment was applied to his last workweek, workweek 4 in which he earned $60, he would receive no paycheck at all for the amount subject to garnishment, $63, is greater than his pay for that week. Again, under the Federal Consumer Credit Protection Act, the total garnishment on workweek number 4 would have only been $25. Obviously the Ohio law when applied in a manner set forth above is less restrictive than the Consumer Credit Protection Act.

Because of the lesser restrictions imposed by the Ohio law if the statute is interpreted as above, and because Ohio does not define specifically enough the term "personal earnings" so as to include pensions and other payments, and because Ohio law is not clear as to the protection afforded non-residents, and because Ohio law is not clear as to whether or not the exemption must be raised affirmatively, the Administrator has denied Ohio's application for exemption.

A review of other state statutes points up similar inconsistencies with the Federal law which will probably result in many denials of exemption. It is anticipated that after several states have tried and failed to obtain exemption from the Federal legislation that uniform legislation among the states, such as suggested by the American Bar Association, will be adopted. Of course, those states which do not in practice recognize wage garnishments, will not have any impetus for adopting such legislation, but those states wishing to preserve the practice in their jurisdictions will find uniform state legislation the most economical and practical way of doing so.

Until uniform legislation is adopted, there will be considerable litigation in every state, which litigation will determine whether or not the state statute can be applied in harmony with the Consumer Credit Protection Act.

Wage Exemptions

Beyond the exemptions provided by the Consumer Credit Protection Act and the various state statutes, there are some basic rules established by judicial decision which are fairly standard throughout the United States and its territories.

Basic to any garnishment or attachment procedure for that matter is the concept that the debtor must have an absolute right to the funds or property. This rule holds true as it pertains to wage garnishments. A creditor cannot subject to garnishment wages, earnings, commissions, pension payments or the like, which have not been earned or are not payable at the time notice of the garnishment is served upon the garnishee. Earnings or wages to be paid upon the contingency or the debtor's promise that certain work will be done in the future are not subject to garnishment before the work is performed. The same rule pertains to commissions or bonuses to be paid upon the completion of work or the meeting of a sales quota.

Likewise, earnings or wages which become due and payable after service of the garnishment notice or writ upon the garnishment are not subject to that garnishment. The creditor would have to refile, within the time prescribed by local law, to reach these subsequent earnings.

There may be situations, however, where future earnings may be subject to garnishment. If, for instance, an employee normally receives his salary in advance each month or other pay period, these earnings may be properly garnished. This does not mean that a casual advance by an employer to an employee not made for the purpose of defrauding, hindering, or delaying a creditor from collecting his just debt, will be subject to wage garnishment. The employee must receive advance payments of earnings on a regular basis so that, in fact, the earnings or wages can be considered as due and payable in advance even though the actual work has not been done.

Some states restrict the garnishment of wages due public officers or employees. On the other hand, some states make no distinctions between public employees and others, although there might be some distinction in the procedure to be followed in accomplishing the garnishment. Ohio, for instance, has in the past required a larger filing fee and an extra copy of the garnishment request to be filed when a creditor sought to garnish the wages of a state employee. This may be extended to teachers who, although they work for the local school districts, are truly employees of the state.

State legislators have been considered to be state officials in some jurisdictions, while police officers are usually considered to be employees of the particular municipality they work for rather than state employees.

In light of these general guidelines, one should consult both the federal legislation and his particular state's legislation to determine what his exposure is as a debtor, or possibilities of collection if he is a creditor.

Scope of Uniform Consumer Credit Code

The Uniform Consumer Credit Code differs from the Consumer Credit Protection Act as its limitations on garnishment apply only to judgments arising from transactions involving consumer sales, consumer loans, and consumer leases.

The Code defines consumer credit sales as those sales of goods or services in which credit is extended by the seller who is one who regularly engages as a seller in credit transactions of the same kind.

The buyer must be a person other than an organization, and the goods and services purchased must be intended for personal, family or household purposes. Further, the debt must be payable in installments or a credit service charge made. The amount financed cannot exceed twenty-five thousand dollars.

Recap of Wage Garnishments

Over the past few years, the process of wage garnishments has evolved from an unstandardized, disoriented procedure to one which must meet Federal and Supreme Court standards. Prejudgment garnishments, effectively, have been eliminated, and the amount of wages which can be taken by a creditor has been substantially reduced, in many instances, by the Consumer Credit Protection Act. Regulations for insuring an orderly, just, and equitable procedure are still left up to the several states, but it is anticipated that application of the Federal legislation and the rules established by the Administrator of the Wage and Hour Division of the Department of Labor will adequately protect a debtor while still allowing a creditor to collect a portion of his claims by use of wage garnishment.

State statutes pertaining to wage garnishments may still take precedent over the Federal law if they are substantially similar to or more restrictive than the Federal provisions. Each state may seek an exemption of its laws from the Federal legislation.

It is hoped that the number of personal bankruptcies will be reduced as the amount of wages taken by garnishment reduces and the number of persons who lose their employment as a result of garnishment declines. An employee cannot be discharged from his employment solely for the reason that his earnings have been subject to garnishment on any one indebtedness.

At this time, the exact interpretation of the new Federal legislation and newly enacted state statutes is still in doubt. As time passes, however, and the courts are given the opportunity to make such interpretations, an orderly process, with some semblance of standardization, will evolve throughout the United States. This writer anticipates a tremendous decline in the number of personal wage garnishments as creditors realize that the amount of wages which can be taken, when considered in light of filing fees, attorney fees and the like, leaves little to apply on the outstanding obligation. Creditors will have to seek other means to satisfy their claims.

Chapter Three

GARNISHMENT -- OTHER THAN WAGES

Generally

Although one usually thinks of wages or other personal earnings being the subject of garnishment, there is a wide range of property which may be taken by garnishment proceedings. Garnishment, of course, differs from the taking of personal property which is in the hands of the debtor, as the process pertains to only those funds or property which can be found in the possession of a third person, that is, someone other than the debtor or creditor. The most customary groupings of such property are bank accounts, both commercial and savings, debts or accounts receivable due to the debtor, equitable interests in trusts and the like, and other funds being held for the benefit of the debtor by diverse persons. Generally, then, any person, firm, partnership, or corporation who holds property of the debtor or who is indebted to the debtor is liable as a garnishee in the garnishment procedure.

The property sought to be taken by garnishment must be owned by the debtor, or the debtor must at least have some legal or equitable interest in it at the time the notice of garnishment is served upon the garnishee. The process is only effective to take that property in the hands of the garnishee at the time of service as it cannot include property coming into the garnishee's possession subsequent to the service of the garnishment order or writ.

Real Property

Generally, all personal property owned by the debtor, limited by applicable exemption statutes, is subject to garnishment. Real property, on the other hand, is usually the subject of foreclosure or other process of execution including attachment. Normally, a debtor's interest in real property is legal title, and since the process of garnishment applies to property in the possession of third persons, it would not be the appropriate procedure to secure the debtor's interest in property to which he has legal title. It may be the appropriate procedure when the real property is titled in the name of another, and it can be shown that the debtor has some equitable interest therein which is ascertainable and definable.

While real property itself cannot usually be the subject of garnishment, the proceeds of sale of such property in the hands of someone other than the debtor, who would be the true owner of those funds, would be fair game for the garnishment procedure. Accrued rents, payable at the time of service of garnishment notice, can be subjected to garnishment as opposed to rents not yet due and payable. Those rents which are not payable at the time garnishment notice is served are still contingent and not absolute.

Bank Accounts

Bank accounts are a prime example of property subject to garnishments other than wages. The title to the funds, of course, is in the depositor while the actual possession of the funds is in the bank. The bank, then, would be the garnishee, the creditor the plaintiff and the depositor the debtor or defendant. Once the garnishment procedure has been initiated, the creditor can be thought of as taking the place of the depositor at least to the extent of his claim against the account.

By garnisheeing the debtor's bank account, the creditor acquires all rights that the debtor had in that account. The garnishee, bank, must then pay such funds to the court out of which came the garnishment order to the extent which the debtor himself may have withdrawn the funds. If the debtor was limited to some extent in his authority to withdrawal, the bank will be limited to the same extent in turning over the funds for the benefit of the creditor. For example, if the debtor is designated as trustee for another on the account, and it can be established that he truly holds the funds in a fiduciary capacity, that is, in a representative capacity for the benefit of another, the garnishee will not be required to turn over the funds.

Perhaps the most complicated problems arise where the debtor holds title to the account jointly with one or more persons.

Such accounts usually specify that either person named on the account may draw without the signature of the other and that upon the death of one, the account in its entirety will pass to the survivor. This type of arrangement, joint and survivorship accounts, has given rise to numerous judicial interpretations usually initiated by third party claims. That is, once the garnishment procedure has been initiated and notice given to the debtor, the person whose name also appears on the account contests the turn over of the funds to apply on the debtor's debt by alleging that the funds contained in the account are in actuality his rather than the debtor's. In such cases, the courts must examine the agreements between the depositors themselves and between the depositors and the bank or other financial institution holding the funds.

Under Minnesota law, it has been held that a joint bank account which gives either party a right to withdrawal of funds is subject to an attachment or garnishment of a creditor of one of the depositors. The entire account, no matter who contributed to it, is susceptible to execution where it cannot be determined precisely who contributed what to the account. On the other hand, where it can be ascertained just how much the debtor contributed to the account, only that portion can be taken by garnishment or other process.

In most cases, if it can be shown that the depositor whose obligation gave rise to the garnishment is not the one who made the contribution to the account, the garnishment can be set aside. The Ohio Supreme Court has held that even though an account is carried in the names of husband and wife and either could draw, the account could not be subjected to garnishment by the husband's creditors where it could be shown that the wife was in reality the sole owner of the funds. She had exclusively contributed the funds to the account.

A debtor depositor can find himself in even deeper trouble when his commercial checking account is garnished. The garnishment applies to the amount contained in the account at the time notice is given or served upon the garnishee. Consequently, any check outstanding at that time will not be covered when presented to the bank. The debtor then finds himself in an embarassing position, to say the least.

Creditors usually begin their search for assets out of which to satisfy their claims by hunting for bank accounts. Banks have no vested interest in a depositor's account and accordingly, are most cooperative in complying with garnishment orders. Exemption statutes which apply to various classifications of property normally have no application to savings or commercial bank accounts. Effectively, then, a debtor has no way of protecting these assets from garnishment.

Life Insurance

Garnishment might even extend as far as one's life insurance policies. Generally, however, the proceeds of life insurance policies are not subject to garnishment as they are contingent upon the death of the insured and therefore are not ascertainable. In some states, life insurance policies can be garnished to the extent of accumulated cash surrender value, loan value or dividends earned.

Most states exempt from garnishment any value of a life policy where the beneficiaries are the surviving spouse and/or children, and several go as far as exempting the proceeds of the policy itself once they are distributed to such beneficiaries.

Many policies of insurance build a cash surrender value or a loan value which can come to the insured or owner of the policy at his option. Some states exempt those values so long as the insured or owner has not exercised his option to surrender the policy or borrow against it.

In the absence of an exemption statute to the contrary, dividends either to be taken in the form of cash payment or to accumulate in the possession of the insurance company can be taken by the insured's creditor through the garnishment process. The insured must have, however, exercised an option to have the dividends distributed or accumulated, as before he does there is no definitive obligation due and owing from the insurance company to the insured on which the creditor may levy. Garnishment can only reach those assets in the hands of a third person which are definite in nature and ascertainable in character.

An annuity policy may provide the creditor with a successful source of garnishment so long as the payments are due and owing the debtor. Contrary to the annuity situation, a fully paid up life insurance policy offers the creditor little opportunity for satisfaction of the obligation owing to him from the insured debtor.

Since the proceeds of the policy will not be paid until the death of the debtor, there is no obligation due him from the insurance company prior to his death. Although the accumulated dividends, cash surrender value and loan value may be subject to garnishment prior to his death, depending on the applicable exemption statute, the proceeds themselves cannot be reached by garnishment or attachment procedures.

Insurance which covers risks other than death, such as fire or liability, builds no value and is only payable upon the happening of the named contingency. Accordingly, there is no value for a creditor to garnishee. Disability benefits under a life policy may be subject to garnishment, in the absence of an exemption statute stating contrary, where the insured's rights to those benefits and the insurance company's obligation to pay same have fully accrued.

Group policies payable in a lump sum or as an annuity upon retirement offer no opportunity to a creditor when the policy expressly contains a provision making the payments thereunder nonassignable.

In some cases, a life insurance policy might contain an option available to the insurer to name the person or entity who will receive the proceeds of the insurance. When this option is included, there can be no garnishment of the proceeds until the insurer has exercised this option.

There has been some judicial interpretation under various state garnishment laws which prohibit the garnishment of cash surrender value of policies unless all of the conditions which the insured would have to perform to get such value for himself have been performed. Generally, there must have been a default in premium payment beyond any grace period; there must have been a surrender of the policy itself; and there must have been a demand made upon the insurance company for payment of the cash surrender value.

Along the same lines, there is authority to the fact that there can be no garnishment of loan values of a policy unless the insured has made application for a loan.

Both these decisions reflect the basics of garnishment. The funds or property sought to be taken must be due and payable to the debtor. Before an insured makes application for a loan on his policy or performs the conditions precedent to payment of the cash surrender value, there is no obligation on the insurance company to pay such sums to him. A creditor can obtain no greater rights in the funds or property than his debtor has.

Chart III sets out the scope of the insurance exemption state-by-state.

CHART III

INSURANCE EXEMPTIONS

State	Exemptions
ALABAMA	Life proceeds are exempt with the exception of the amount attributable to premium paid with the intent to defraud creditors.
ALASKA	General exemption for insurance proceeds.
ARIZONA	Proceeds of life, fire and other property insurance is exempt.
ARKANSAS	General exemption for insurance proceeds.
CALIFORNIA	Proceeds of life, disability, and health insurance exempt, subject to a maximum measured by yearly premiums.
COLORADO	Proceeds of life insurance exempt up to a maximum of $5,000.
CONNECTICUT	Proceeds of life insurance exempt if the named beneficiary is someone other than the insured.
DELAWARE	Life insurance proceeds are exempt except as they are attributable to premiums paid to drfraud creditors.

CHART III (continued)

State	Exemption
DISTRICT OF COLUMBIA	Proceeds of life insurance on a husband is exempt if wife is the beneficiary.
FLORIDA	Life insurance proceeds are exempt except those attributable to premiums paid to defraud creditors. Disability proceeds also exempt.
GEORGIA	Proceeds of life insurance exempt except those funds related to premiums paid to defraud creditors.
HAWAII	Proceeds of life, endowment or annuity policies exempt, if the beneficiary of the life policy is the wife and the beneficiaries of the others are either husband, wife, child, or parent.
IDAHO	Proceeds are exempt up to an amount generated by annual premiums not exceeding $250.
ILLINOIS	Life proceeds are exempt with the exception of the amount attributable to premiums paid with the intent to defraud creditors.
INDIANA	Life proceeds are exempt except those attributable to premiums paid to defraud creditors.
IOWA	Proceeds of life and accident policies are exempt if payable to husband, wife, or children. If such proceeds are payable to widow, the policy is exempt before the insured's death to an amount not in excess of $15,000.

CHART III (continued)

State	Exemption
KANSAS	Proceeds are exempt except those earned by premiums made to defraud creditors.
KENTUCKY	General exemption except as to proceeds attributable to premiums paid to defraud creditors.
LOUISIANA	Proceeds of life, health and accident policies are exempt as to those debts secured by a pledge of the policy.
MAINE	General exemption except as to those proceeds attributable to premiums paid to defraud creditors.
MARYLAND	Proceeds of both life and accident policies are exempt.
MASSACHUSETTS	Life proceeds are exempt to the extent they do not reflect premiums paid to defraud creditors. Disability proceeds exempt, except as to debts arising from necessaries purchased.
MICHIGAN	General exemption except as to those proceeds attributable to premiums paid to defraud creditors.
MINNESOTA	Life proceeds payable to wife and/or children of the insured are exempt, up to $10,000. Proceeds from risk to exempt property, also exempt.
MISSISSIPPI	Proceeds of life insurance exempt up to $10,000. If the beneficiary of the policy is the fiduciary of the insured's estate, the proceeds are exempt up to $5,000.

CHART III (continued)

State	Exemption
MISSOURI	Proceeds of life insurance payable to wife on husband's death is exempt.
MONTANA	Life insurance proceeds are exempt up to an amount attributable to annual premiums of $500.
NEBRASKA	Life insurance proceeds are exempt up to an amount attributable to annual premiums of $500.
NEVADA	Life insurance proceeds are exempt to the extent they are attributable to annual premiums of no more than $500.
NEW HAMPSHIRE	Proceeds payable to wife and/or children are exempt.
NEW JERSEY	General exemption except as those proceeds attributable to premium payments made to defraud creditors.
NEW MEXICO	The cash surrender value of life insurance policies is exempt.
NEW YORK	Proceeds are exempt except to the extent they are attributable to premiums paid to defraud creditors. Annuity payments are exempt except as to the excess of such payments over an amount necessary for the education and support of the family.
NORTH CAROLINA	Proceeds of insurance exempt except that portion attributable to premiums paid with the intent to defraud creditors.

CHART III (continued)

State	Exemption
OHIO	Proceeds and cash surrender value of policies on which the beneficiary is the spouse, children, or relative dependent on the insured are exempt.
OKLAHOMA	General exemption except those proceeds attributable to premiums paid with the intent to defraud creditors.
OREGON	Proceeds exempt except those attributable to premiums paid with the intent to defraud creditors.
PENNSYLVANIA	Proceeds of life insurance policies exempt if the named beneficiary is the wife, children, or dependent relative. Proceeds of accident and disability policies are exempt. Proceeds held by the insurance company pursuant to agreement containing nonassignment clause are exempt.
RHODE ISLAND	Proceeds are exempt up to amount attributable to premiums not paid with the intent to defraud creditors.
SOUTH CAROLINA	Proceeds are exempt up to amount attributable to yearly premiums of $500 provided the named beneficiary is the wife, her heirs, or the children and their heirs.
SOUTH DAKOTA	Proceeds of life insurance exempt up to $10,000 if the proceeds are payable to the husband, wife, or children. Proceeds of endowment policies up to $10,000 are exempt.

CHART III (continued)

State	Exemption
TENNESSEE	Life proceeds exempt if wife or children are the beneficiaries. Annuity payment to wife or children or dependent relative are exempt.
TEXAS	Cash surrender value of life policies which have been in force for more than two years is exempt if the beneficiary is a member of the insured's family.
UTAH	Life proceeds are exempt to the extent they are attributable to no more than $500 in annual premium payments.
VERMONT	The beneficiary for whose benefit the policy has been made has the best claim as against any creditor of the insured.
VIRGINIA	Only fraternal benefits are exempt.
WASHINGTON	Proceeds are exempt except to the extent they are attributable to premium payments made with the intent to defraud creditors. Accident and health proceeds are exempt.
WEST VIRGINIA	Proceeds payable to a married woman are exempt except as to those proceeds attributable to premium payments made in excess of $300 and with the intent to defraud creditors.
WISCONSIN	Those proceeds exceeding $150 per month are not exempt. Generally, all others are with the exception of those attributable to premium payments made with the intent to defraud creditors.

CHART III (continued)

State	Exemption
WYOMING	General exemption except as to those proceeds attributable to premium payments made with the intent to defraud creditors.

Partnership Property

The area of partnership law offers many possibilities for complex problems involving attachment or garnishment. What rights do creditors of the individual partners have against partnership property? What rights do creditors of the partnership have against property of the individual partners? What rights do the creditors of an individual partner have as against the property of other partners?

The Uniform Partnership Act as adopted by states answers most of the questions above posed. Section 25(1)(c) of that act provides in substance that since a partner is a co-owner of the partnership property, his right in specific partnership property cannot be subjected to attachment or garnishment except by virtue of a claim against the partnership as opposed to a claim against an individual partner. In other words, no partner owns an ascertainable portion of a specific asset held by the partnership. No one partner can say that a specific portion of a specific machine or land is his. Accordingly, the creditors of the individual partners cannot attach or garnish a specific portion of any partnership asset by reason of a debt due and owing from an individual partner. Only the creditors of the partnership can invoke such remedies against the assets of the partnership.

It is interesting to note that the Uniform Partnership Act further provides that in the event partnership property is levied upon by any process including garnishment or attachment that the individual partners or their representatives are excluded from invoking any right under the exemption statutes which might otherwise be available to them, including the homestead exemption of real property.

Since all partners are jointly responsible for the acts or omissions of the other partners (unless excluded by the partnership agreement), one partner might find his personal property being taken to satisfy a debt incurred by another partner in connection with the operation of the partnership. Individual property of one partner cannot, however, be subjected to garnishment or attachment or other legal process where the creditor seeking to invoke such remedy is the individual creditor of another partner and the act or omission which gave rise to the obligation ocurred outside the scope of partnership activity.

While a creditor of an individual partner cannot subject partnership property to garnishment or other process, he can subject a partner's interest in the partnership as an entity. Just as a debtor's stock holdings in a corporation can be taken to satisfy an obligation, the partner's interest in the partnership as measured by his share of the surplus remaining after payment of partnership liabilities and settlement of partnership accounts can be subjected to legal process.

Since the Uniform Partnership Act has been adopted by numerous states, the rules of attachment and garnishment pertaining thereto are reasonably clear.

Equitable Interests

Unlike partnership property, equitable interests in property is an area where there is no uniform legislation. Equitable interests are not often subject to the garnishment process because of their indefiniteness. Since garnishment is a creature of statute, the statute in question must expressly allow garnishment of equitable interests such as those derived from trusts or estates before a creditor is able to use such process on that type of property.

It might be well to explain here that an equitable interest differs from legal interest or title. An equitable interest in property is some right or claim upon property whose legal title is vested in another. For example, the trustee is the legal title holder of the property being held in trust. The beneficiary for whose benefit the trustee holds title has an equitable interest in the trust and its property.

In those states that do allow the attachment or garnishment of equitable interests in real or personal property, it is axiomatic that the interest of the debtor must be absolute and definable as opposed to being uncertain or resting on some contingency. The interest must be an absolute right in a beneficiary, for instance, to receive income from a trust before the beneficiary's creditor can invoke the garnishment process. The trustee would, of course, be the garnishee and required to turn over the funds due to the beneficiary under the terms of the trust if the beneficiary's interest is certain and not dependent on any contingency.

In many trusts the turstee has been vested with discretion as to how much and how frequently the beneficiary is to be paid out of the trust income or trust property which produces that income. When the turstee has been vested with such discretion, the beneficiary's interest becomes contingent and unascertainable. Accordingly, the beneficiary's interest in the possession of the trust would not be subject to garnishment.

Several states recognize what is commonly called spendthrift trusts or spendthrift provisions. This type of trust prohibits the beneficiary from anticipatorily alienating his equitable interest in the trust. That is, he cannot assign such interest or otherwise encumber it prior to acutal distribution of the funds from the trustee to himself. Those states which allow such trusts logically do not allow the garnishment of such equitable interests in the hands of the trustee. Some jurisdictions, however, do allow the garnishment against the funds of a spendthrift trust to the extent those funds are over and above what is needed for the support and maintenance of the beneficiary.

Since the trustee is the legal title holder of the trust property, it might appear that a trustee's creditor could reach the trust property by means of levying execution. This is not, however, the case, as a trustee's creditor cannot have his claim satisfied out of property being held in trust for another.

Beyond the normal trust situation, equitable interests may exist in trusts implied by law such as where one provides another with the funds to purchase property in the latter's name. Although there is no contract establishing the equitable interest, it is nevertheless in existence. Where the statute provides for the garnishment of equitable interests an interest implied by law may be taken. If a series of questions arises as to the debtor's interest in the property, it may be necessary for the creditor to institute what is commonly known as a "Creditor's Bill." In this particular type of action, a court is asked to determine whether or not a third person having legal title to property is, in fact, holding such property for the benefit of the debtor. If it is found that the debtor does have such an equitable interest in the property, it will be ordered turned over to the creditor. The end result, then, is the same as if a garnishment order had been honored.

A prerequisite to this type of action usually is the creditor's unsuccessful attempt at customary execution procedures.

Equitable interests, then, are not exempt from a creditor's claim. Although the exact procedure may differ from jurisdiction to jurisdiction, the availability of such assets to creditors is almost universal.

Decedent's Estates

Most states do not allow the garnishment of a beneficiary's interest in a decedent's estate prior to distribution or settlement of the estate. After final determination of the amount due the beneficiary, but before actual distribution of the funds, the fiduciary, representative of the estate, is usually subject to garnishment. At that time he is no longer holding the funds or property as an officer of the court, but rather as a personal debtor of the beneficiary. A creditor of the beneficiary would, then, be able to garnish this obligation.

A creditor of the decedent's estate is not, in most states, vested with the right to attach or garnish assets of the estate in the hands of the fiduciary. Most states provide specific procedures whereby a decedent's creditor can process his claim. To allow creditors to levy execution would be preferential treatment and would, in most cases, mean that the first creditor to exercise that prerogative would receive his funds to the obvious detriment of the remaining creditors.

While some states allow the garnishment of estate assets before an order of distribution has gone on, the logic in excluding such seems to be the better reasoning. Before the order has been made, the beneficiary debtor has no present right to the funds or property. The beneficiary's interest in the estate is uncertain, to say the least, and is contingent upon the order being approved by the probate court without objection or attack by the creditors of the decedent.

Those states which do allow pre-distribution order garnishments are not in absolute accord as to the extent of taking available to the creditor. Some states are very lenient and allow the creditors to reach both real and personal property of the estate which would have eventually been distributed to his debtor, the beneficiary. Others allow the taking of personal property only.

The attachment statutes of New Jersey permit the sequestering of a decedent's property by a creditor when the claim is of the type which survives the death of the debtor. That is, the claim does not abate when the defendant dies. As a further qualification for such purposes, however, the heirs or fiduciary or any one of them must be a nonresident of the state.

After the order of distribution has been made, there is no question but that garnishment can be used to reach the debtor's legacy; that is, unless there is an explicit state statute to the contrary.

Stock

Corporate stock generally may not be taken by garnishment procedures. Such interest may, however, be reached under special statutes which will not be considered at this point.

Pensions

Government pensions and the like while in the hands of the government, be it Federal, state or local, cannot be subjected to garnishment. If a pensioner has directed that payments be made to a third person, those proceeds in the hands of the third person would be vulnerable to garnishment process.

While pension payments from a private employer may be taken by garnishment when they become due, if the terms of the pension plan provide that the benefits are not assignable, the funds will be protected from garnishment.

It is important to recall, when speaking of the susceptibility of pension payments to garnishments, that the Consumer Credit Protection Act includes such payments in its limitation provisions. The reason for this inclusion is obvious. A person relying upon a fixed income such as a pension should not be totally deprived of such income any more than a wage earner should be deprived of all his earnings.

Chapter Four

GARNISHMENT PROCEDURE

A creditor seeking to satisfy a claim against a debtor by means of garnishment of either wages or other property must follow the rules and regulations established by state statute or local court rule. Although the exact procedures differ between states and, in fact, between jurisdictions within individual states, the primary features are usually similar.

As previously discussed, there are three parties to a garnishment procedure. The creditor is the plaintiff, the principal debtor is the defendant, and the person holding funds belonging to the debtor or owing money to the debtor is called the garnishee.

Garnishment procedures can be invoked in the same case by which the creditor established his claim against the debtor or it may be a separate action altogether, depending on the particular jurisdiction. In any event, the procedure is usually started by the filing of a petition accompanied by an affidavit. The creditor or his agent or attorney must state under oath that there is a certain sum due to the creditor which sum is derived from a judgment rendered on a particular day and that the judgment is wholly or partially unsatisfied. The affiant, person making the affidavit, must further state the name and address of the garnishee and the type of property that the garnishee is holding on behalf of the debtor. Most states or local jurisdictions require a further statement that the funds or property sought to be garnished are not exempt from garnishment by virtue of the state constitution or statute.

Subsequent to the original filing of the petition or affidavit along with the prescribed filing fees, the court will issue an order of garnishment sometimes called a writ of garnishment. This order or writ will then be served upon the garnishee in a means prescribed by statute. In most cases it will be by mail service as opposed to personal hand delivery, but the mode of service often differs between courts in the same state.

The order or writ is often simply an approved copy of the original petition or complaint, having been completed by an officer of the court as to the date and time by which the garnishee must answer or appear in court.

The purpose, of course, of completing service on the garnishee is to put him on notice that he is required to answer within the stated time. Likewise, the principal debtor is usually served with a copy of the garnishment order or writ to put him on notice that the procedure has been instituted. Some states do nor require that the principal debtor be notified of the procedure, so it is imperative that the particular statute involved be studied to determine the service requirements and the effect of failing to comply therewith.

Once the service requirements have been compiled with, the next procedural step is the responsibility of the garnishee. He must answer by setting forth either an admission or denial that he holds funds, property, or earnings of the principal debtor. A typical answer of a garnishee who is the employer of the debtor might set forth the amount of wages being held at the time of service, or it might state that there are no funds payable, or it might set forth the fact that the debtor is no longer employed by the garnishee.

If the garnishee is required to actually appear in open court on a particular day, he must answer all questions put to him regarding the funds or property he holds on behalf of the debtor. In lieu of appearing, the garnishee may often simply turn over any funds or property to the court along with an answer under oath stating that the funds or property turned over comprise the total of what he held on behalf of the principal debtor at the time the garnishment order or writ was served upon him.

Practically speaking, once a garnishee has been served, for example, the XYZ Bank, it will file an answer setting forth the amount of funds it holds. Upon receipt of the answer and without actual court appearance, the court will order a turn over of those funds. XYZ Bank will comply with the order and the amount turned over will be applied to the creditor's claim.

If the garnishee fails to answer for one reason or another, some states allow the taking of a default judgment against the garnishee. The only effect of this entry would be to initiate further action whereby the rights and obligations of the garnishee would be finally determined. It is simply a means to accomplish the end of having the garnishee disclose the funds or property it holds on behalf of the debtor.

In rare instances, a garnishee might appear and in an attempt to protect the principal debtor, give false information. Some jurisdictions allow the creditor to maintain an action against the garnishee based upon fraud. There is always the possibility that the garnishee could be held in contempt of court for failure to answer or for giving false information upon examination.

Along with the disclosure of the funds or property the garnishee holds in favor of the debtor, the garnishee may set up in his answer any defenses to the garnishment action that he might have. Some states permit the garnishee to bring up as a defense on his own behalf any defense that the principal debtor had against the creditor. Of course, in garnishment procedures after judgment it can reasonably be assumed that the debtor asserted any defenses he may have had in the principal action before judgment was rendered. By way of defense, the garnishee might assert that he has already paid over the funds or turned over the property to the principal debtor before he was served with notice of the garnishment.

Most states allow or even encourage the garnishee to set up as a partial defense, the exemptions allowable to the debtor. This is especially true when wages or other earnings are the subject of the garnishment. Depending upon the particular statute, it may be the express obligation of the garnishee to set up the exemption, or he may have no obligation to do so.

A garnishee's obligation and responsibility extends only to the funds or property he holds on behalf of the debtor. Normally, the garnishee is not responsible for court costs and some courts award a small stipend to the garnishee to cover a portion of his costs incurred in additional bookkeeping and the like. If, however, the garnishee denies that there are any funds or property in his possession belonging to the debtor, he may be responsible for costs of the proceedings if it is finally determined that such funds or property did exist at the time of service of the garnishment.

Garnishment procedure may be cut short or terminated by the debtor's payment to the creditor. In that event, the creditor will issue a release to the debtor which release will, upon presentation to the court, terminate that particular garnishment proceeding. The giving of a release on one garnishment proceeding does not prevent the creditor from initiating subsequent proceedings if the debtor fails to make further payments as may have been agreed upon.

The steps outlined above apply both to the garnishment of wages and other property. In the case of wage garnishment, most states require the sending of a statutory demand to the debtor before the affidavit or petition can be filed with the court. The particulars of this notice were discussed earlier, but it is important to reiterate the necessity of such notice as it gives the debtor a fair opportunity to make arrangements for payment to the creditor before the actual garnishment procedure is instituted.

Like all types of suits, garnishments must be properly filed and actions thereafter must comply with both the state statutes and local rules. Failure of a creditor to so comply can result in a dismissal of the proceeding.

Chapter Five

ATTACHMENT

Generally

Unlike the remedy of garnishment, attachment occurs previous to the taking of judgment against an alleged debtor. Unlike garnishment, attachment pertains to property in the possession of the debtor and within the territorial jurisdiction of the court in which the creditor seeks to enforce his rights against the debtor.

The proceeding known as attachment originated in England and existed in the English common law. It was a means by which a tradesman could satisfy the debts owing to him. The English common law as it was adopted in the United States traditionally required a defendant to be within the jurisdiction of the court before the court would act. Here it is important to understand that there are two types of jurisdiction which a court may obtain. The first is in "persona" jurisdiction, or personal jurisdiction over the person of the debtor. The second is jurisdiction "in rem," or jurisdiction over property. Attachment falls somewhere between the two and is often called a "quasi rem proceeding."

Under the English common law if, after having been served with summons, a defendant failed to respond for one reason or another, a writ of attachment could be issued and his property seized. The purpose of the seizure, however, was not to secure a fund out of which the creditor's claim could be satisfied, but rather to compel the appearance of the defendant. If he fails to appear, the property cannot be held for the benefit of the creditor but rather forfeited to the state. If, after learning of the seizure of his property, the debtor appears for purposes of suit, the goods or property will return to him and not be held as security for the plaintiff's claim.

As the law evolved in England, the forfeited property of a debtor while still being forfeited to the state, was also used to satisfy the costs of the action that the creditor had incurred.

As the law evolved further and was applied in the Lord Mayor's Court in London, attachment began to reach not only the tangible goods of the defendant within the territorial jurisdiction of the court, but also debts owed to the defendant by third persons. This, of course, would fall under the heading of a garnishment proceeding but importantly, that property now began to inure to the benefit of the creditor in the event that the debtor did not make an appearance for purposes of suit. Once the property was attached, the court then had jurisdiction to render a verdict against the defendant without his having to appear. The scope of the jurisdiction acquired by this type of proceeding, however, is limited to the value of the attached property or res which constitutes the basis of in rem jurisdiction.

The earliest attachment laws in the United States were enacted in Pennsylvania in 1705 and in New Jersey in 1798. These laws primarily followed the general pattern of attachment statutes as we know them today. The main objective of those statutes and of the statutes on the books today is to reach the property of the defendant in order to secure a fund for the satisfaction of the creditor's demand.

Attachment may be thought of as a provisional remedy, the nature of which is to levy execution of goods owned by the defendant in anticipation of the establishment of the plaintiff's claim in the primary action. A writ of attachment may be thought of as an execution in advance of judgment. Attachment is an extraordinary remedy in that the rights of a party may be determined without service of process upon him and perhaps even without his knowledge. It is a statutory proceeding ancillary to the main action in which the creditor tries to establish his claim against the debtor.

Most courts throughout the United States have required that precise and definite allegations which meet both the letter and the spirit of the attachment law must be made in order to satisfy the issuance of a writ of attachment.

Without, at this point, enumerating the various grounds for attachments which are contained in most of the state statutes, a common ground is that the debtor is a nonresident who possesses property in the state in which the creditor resides. Again, the reason for being able to attach nonresident's property is that he cannot be brought into court by means of personal service. By allowing the attachment of his property within the territorial jurisdiction of the court where the action is brought, the debtor is placed in a position of equality as far as being subject to suit, with other residents of the state.

To date, there has been no Federal widesweeping legislation affecting the rights of a creditor to attach a debtor's property, but each state has set forth its own statute which allows or disallows the attachment before judgment and which removes certain property from subjection to attachment.

Most states limit an attachment proceeding to actions upon contract either express or implied and unsecured by mortgage or security interest in a particular chattel. Most states do not allow attachment of goods or property prior to the initiation of a suit involving an alleged tort or negligent act or omission on the part of the alleged debtor causing personal injury or property damage to the creditor.

A complete list of the grounds for attachment in various states can be found in Chart IV, but most states in general require that the defendant be a nonresident or that there be an element of fraud or concealment of assets from the jurisdiction of the court before an attachment can be granted.

While each one of the grounds set out in Chart IV may seem obvious on its face, each is subject to judicial interpretation and there is a myriad of cases in every jurisdiction interpreting each one of the grounds contained in the particular state statute.

CHART IV

GROUNDS FOR ATTACHMENT -- STATE STATUTES

<u>ALABAMA</u>
1. Defendant is a non-resident.
2. Defendant has absconded.
3. Defendant has secreted himself.
4. Defendant is about to leave the state.
5. Defendant is about to remove his property from the state.
6. Defendant is about to fraudulently dispose of his property.

CHART IV (continued)

ALABAMA (cont'd.)
7. Defendant has fraudulently disposed of his property.
8. Defendant is fraudulently withholding funds or property.

ALASKA
1. In any action on a contract for the payment of money when such contract is not secured of if secured, the security is insufficient to satisfy the debt.
2. The defendant is a non-resident and the action is one on contract.
3. The action is for collection of any state tax or license fee.

ARIZONA

Debt Not Due
1. Contract of obligation is unsecured.
2. Defendant is about to remove himself from the state.
3. Defendant secreted property to defraud creditors.
4. Defendant disposed of or is about to remove property with intent to defraud creditors.

Debt Due
1. The contract of obligation, express or implied, is not fully secured.
2. Defendant is a non-resident.
3. Defendant is a foreign corporation.
4. An executor or administrator failed to file a verified account.
5. The obligation is upon a judgment of any state or District of Columbia.

ARKANSAS
1. Defendant is a foreign corporation or non-resident.
2. Defendant has been absent from the state for four months.

CHART IV (continued)

ARKANSAS (cont'd.)
3. Defendant departed with the intent to defraud creditors.
4. Defendant left his county of residence or secretes himself to avoid service of summons.
5. Defendant is about to or has removed his property.
6. Defendant has sold or conveyed his property with the intention of defrauding creditors.

CALIFORNIA
1. That the action is upon contract express or implied and unsecured.
2. Defendant is a non-resident.
3. Defendant has departed the state.
4. Defendant conceals himself.
5. Defendant is a non-resident or person concealing himself who has injured property by negligence, fraud or other wrongful act.
6. The action is one for rent, unsecured by mortgage or lien.
7. The state or local government is attempting to collect taxes or other obligations imposed by law.

COLORADO
1. Defendant is a non-resident.
2. Defendant is a foreign corporation.
3. Defendant is a domestic corporation having its cheif office out of the state.
4. Defendant conceals himself or has been absent for four months.
5. Defendant removed property with intent to defraud creditors.
6. Defendant fraudulently conveyed or concealed property to delay creditors.

CHART IV (continued)

COLORADO (cont'd.)
7. Defendant departed from the state intent to remove his property.
8. Defendant refused to pay the price of articles delivered or work done.
9. Defendant fraudulently contracted the debt or procured money or property fraudulently.

CONNECTICUT
There are no special grounds. Any action for the recovery of money except actions for slander, libel or invasion of privacy may be started by attachment.

DELAWARE
Generally any action in contract or tort may be initiated by an attachment.

DISTRICT OF COLUMBIA
1. Defendant is a foreign corporation or non-resident.
2. Defendant has been absent for six months.
3. Defendant is evading service of process.
4. Defendant removed or is about to remove property to defeat creditor's claims.
5. Defendant assigned or secreted property or is about to do so to defraud creditors.
6. Defendant fraudulently contracted the debt.

FLORIDA
When Debt is Due
1. Defendant will fraudulently part with property.
2. Defendant is removing his property from the state.
3. Defendant is about to remove his property from the state.

CHART IV (continued)

FLORIDA (cont'd.)
4. Defendant resides out of the state.
5. Defendant is moving or is about to move from the state.
6. Defendant is absconding or concealing himself.
7. Defendant is secreting or disposing of his property.

When Debt Is Not Due
1. Defendant is removing his property from the state.
2. Defendant is fraudulently disposing of his property.
3. Defendant is secreting his property.

GEORGIA
1. Defendant is a non-resident.
2. Defendant is removing or about to remove himself from the county.
3. Defendant has absconded or concealed himself.
4. Defendant has resisted arrest.
5. Defendant is removing property from the state.

HAWAII
Any action on an express or implied contract including those actions brought by non-residents or foreign corporations may be instituted by attachment.

IDAHO
1. In any action on a contract express or implied not secured or if secured, the property has become valueless.
2. Defendant is a non-resident.

ILLINOIS
1. Defendant is a non-resident.
2. Defendant concelas himself to avoid service of summons.

CHART IV (continued)

ILLINOIS (cont'd.)
3. Defendant departed from the state with the intent of having his property so removed.
4. Defendant is about to depart from the state with intention of having his property so removed.
5. Defendant is about to remove his property to the injury of creditors.
6. Defendant has within two years fraudulently conveyed or assigned his property so as to hinder or delay his creditors.
7. Defendant has within two years fraudulently concealed or disposed of property to hinder or delay creditors.
8. Defendant is about to fraudulently conceal, assign or otherwise dispose of property so as to hinder or delay creditors.
9. The debt was fraudulently contracted.

INDIANA
1. Defendant is a foreign corporation or non-resident.
2. Defendant has secreted himself.
3. Defendant is about to leave the state.
4. Defendant is removing property from the state.
5. Defendant has sold or is about to dispose of property with the intent to defraud creditors.
6. Defendant's residence or whereabouts is unknown.

IOWA
1. Defendant is a foreign corporation.
2. Defendant is about to remove his property.

CHART IV (continued)

IOWA (cont'd.)
3. Defendant disposed of or is about to dispose of property with the intent to defraud creditors.
4. Defendant has absconded.
5. Defendant has removed himself and his property.
6. Defendant has removed his property.
7. Defendant has converted or concealed property.

KANSAS
1. Defendant is a non-resident or foreign corporation.
2. Defendant absconded or concealed himself.
3. Defendant is about to remove himself from the state.
4. Defendant is about to remove property from the state.
5. Defendant is about to convert property into money to put it beyond the reach of creditors.
6. Defendant has concealed, removed, assigned or conveyed property to hinder or delay creditors.
7. The debt was fraudulently contracted.
8. Damages sought are for injuries from defendant's commission of a felony, misdemeanor or seduction of a female.
9. Defendant failed to pay the price for articles delivered.

KENTUCKY
1. Defendant is a non-resident or foreign corporation.
2. Defendant has been absent for four months.

CHART IV (continued)

KENTUCKY (cont'd.)
3. Defendant departed with intent to defraud creditors.
4. Defendant left the county to avoid service.
5. Defendant conceals himself.
6. Defendant is about to remove his property.
7. Defendant sold, conveyed, or disposed of property with intent to defraud creditors, or is about to do so.

LOUISIANA
1. In a suit filed by the State of Louisiana or any parish or subdivision thereof or by any public corporation.
2. Where such suit is against a corporation or individual to recover money or property obtained through fraud and;
3. Defendant has the power to mortgage, assign or dispose of his property or can convert such into money or evidences of debt and;
4. Defendant must further be about to dispose, mortgage, assign or convert property with intent to defraud creditors or put property beyond their reach.

MAINE

Attachment may be had in any action in which claim, exclusive of costs, is twenty dollars or more.

MARYLAND
1. Defendant is a non-resident.
2. Defendant is a corporation having no agent but where attempts to serve him have been unsuccessful.

CHART IV (continued)

MARYLAND (cont'd.)
3. Defendant is a resident on whom two attempts at service have failed.
4. Defendant absconded or is about to or removed himself or is about to remove himself from his place of abode with intent to defraud creditors.
5. Defendant fraudulently contracted the debt or obligation.
6. Land of a decedent in the hands of a devisee may be attached.

MASSACHUSETTS

No grounds need be stated.

MICHIGAN
1. Defendant has absconded or is about to do so or is concealed.
2. Defendant assigned, disposed of or concealed any of his property with intention of defrauding creditors.
3. Defendant is about to assign, dispose of or conceal his property.
4. Defendant has removed or is about to remove property from the state with the intent to defraud creditors.
5. Defendant fraudulently contracted the debt or fraudulently incurred the obligation.
6. Defendant is not a resident of the state and has not resided therein for three months.
7. Defendant is a foreign corporation.

MINNESOTA
1. The debt was fraudulently contracted.
2. Defendant is a foreign corporation or a non-resident.
3. Defendant departed the state or concealed himself to avoid services or to defraud creditors.

CHART IV (continued)

MISSISSIPPI
1. Defendant is a foreign corporation or a non-resident.
2. Defendant removed himself or property or is about to do so.
3. Defendant absconds or conceals himself to avoid service.
4. The debt was incurred in conducting the business of a water craft in navigable waters of the state.
5. Defendant conceals or refuses to apply property to the debt.
6. Defendant assigned or disposed of property with intent to defraud creditors or is about to do so.
7. Defendant converted property to money to put it beyond the reach of creditors.
8. The debt was fraudulently contracted.
9. Defendant is buying, selling, or dealing in futures or has done so within the last six months.
10. The debt is due the state or sub-division thereof.
11. Defendant is a banker, banking company or corporation which received deposits while insolvent, or has given false statements as to financial condition.

MISSOURI
1. Defendant is a non-resident.
2. Defendant is a foreign corporation.
3. Defendant conceals himself to avoid service of summons.
4. Defendant has absconded or absented himself from his usual place of abode.
5. Defendant has removed his property with intent to defraud creditors.

CHART IV (continued)

MISSOURI (cont'd.)

6. Defendant is about to leave the state and change his domicile.
7. Defendant has fraudulently conveyed or assigned his property with the intent of defrauding creditors.
8. Defendant has fraudulently concealed, removed or disposed of his property with intent to defraud creditors.
9. Defendant is about to fraudulently convey or assign property to hinder, delay or defraud creditors.
10. Defendant is about to fraudulently conceal or remove or dispose of his property.
11. Where the cause of action accrued out of the state and defendant has absconded, or secretly removed his property into this state.
12. Where the damages sought arose out of defendant's commission of a felony, misdemeanor, or his seduction of any female.
13. Where the debtor has failed to pay the price or value of any article or thing delivered which by contract he was bound to pay upon delivery.
14. Where the defendant fraudulently contracted the debt.

MONTANA

Attachment is available in any action in contract, express or implied, for the direct payment of money where the contract is unsecured, or the security has become valueless.

Action upon statutory stockholders liability.

CHART IV (continued)

NEBRASKA

Debt Is Due

1. Defendant is a foreign corporation or non-resident.
2. Defendant absconded with intent to defraud creditors.
3. Defendant left the county to avoid service.
4. Defendant conceals himself.
5. Defendant is about to remove, or convert property to defraud creditors or put it beyond their reach.
6. Defendant concealed, assigned, removed or disposed of property with intent to defraud creditors or is about to do so.
7. The debt was fraudulently contracted.

Debt Not Due

1. Defendant sold, conveyed property with intent to defraud creditors.
2. Defendant is about to remove property.

NEVADA

1. Defendant absconded or is about to do so with intent of defrauding creditors.
2. Defendant conceals himself.
3. Defendant assigned, removed, or disposed of property with the intent to defraud creditors, or is about to do so.
4. Defendant converted his property to put it beyond the reach of creditors.
5. The debt was fraudulently contracted.

NEW HAMPSHIRE

Generally allowed as a means of initiating an action.

CHART IV (continued)

NEW JERSEY

1. Where the fact would entitle the plaintiff to an order of arrest before judgment in a civil case.
2. Where the defendant has absconded or is a non-resident.
3. Where a cause of action existed against a decedent which action survives against the decedent's heirs, devisees, executors, administrators or trustees and any of such persons are non-residents.
4. In equitable claims where the defendant has absconded or is a non-resident.
5. Defendant is a foreign corporation but authorized to do business in the state.

NEW MEXICO

1. Defendant is a non-resident.
2. Defendant concealed himself or can't be served.
3. Defendant removed, assigned, concealed or disposed of property with intent of defrauding creditors or is about to do so.
4. Defendant is a corporation whose principal place of business is out of the state and has no statutory agent in the state.
5. The debt was fraudulently contracted.
6. The debt is for work, labor, or services requested by the defendant.
7. The debt is for necessities of life.

NEW YORK

1. Defendant is a foreign corporation or a non-resident.
2. Defendant is a resident but can't be served.

CHART IV (continued)

NEW YORK (cont'd.)

3. Defendant departed or keeps himself hidden.
4. Defendant assigned, disposed, or secreted property with intent to defraud creditors.
5. The debt was fraudulently contracted.
6. The debt arose from wrongful receipt, conversion or detention of property held or owned by any governmental agency.
7. Debt is due on judgment from another state.

NORTH CAROLINA

1. Defendant is a non-resident, foreign corporation, or domestic corporation whose officers can't be found.
2. Defendant, with intent to defraud creditors, departed the state, concealed himself, removed, assigned, disposed of, or secreted property, or is about to do so.

NORTH DAKOTA

1. Defendant is a non-resident or foreign corporation.
2. Defendant absconded or concealed himself.
3. Defendant sold, assigned, secreted, disposed, or removed property with the intent of defrauding creditors.
4. Defendant is about to remove property.
5. Defendant incurred the debt under false pretenses.
6. The action is for recovery of purchase price for personal property sold to defendant.

CHART IV (continued)

NORTH DAKOTA (continued)

7. In an action against the owner of a motor vehicle for damages as a result of negligence, the motor vehicle may be attached.

OHIO

1. Defendant is a non-resident.
2. Defendant has absconded to defraud creditors.
3. Defendant left to avoid service of summons.
4. Defendant is about to remove property to defraud creditors.
5. Defendant is about to convert property to defraud creditors.
6. Defendant is concealing property.
7. Defendant has or is about to assign, remove or dispose of his property.
8. Defendant has fraudulently or criminally contracted the debt.
9. The claim is for work, labor or necessaries.
10. Defendant has violated the Bulk Sales Act.

OKLAHOMA

1. Defendant is a foreign corporation or non-resident.
2. Defendant absconded, left the county or conceals himself to avoid service.
3. Defendant removed, converted, assigned, disposed of or concealed property with intent to hinder, delay or defraud creditors or is about to do so.
4. The debt was fraudulently contracted.
5. The debt arose from the commission of a felony, misdemeanor, or seduction of a female.
6. Defendant failed to pay the price of goods delivered.

CHART IV (continued)

OREGON
1. The action is one on contract where the creditor is unsecured or the debtor is a non-resident.
2. The action is one on breach of contract against a non-resident.
3. The action is one against a non-resident for injury to property.

PENNSYLVANIA
1. Defendant has absconded from his usual place of abode.
2. Defendant has remained absent from the common wealth.
3. Defendant has confined himself in his own house.
4. Defendant has concealed himself with the design to defraud creditors.

RHODE ISLAND

Civil Actions
1. Plaintiff has a just claim against the defendant, which claim is due.
2. The amount of the claim is sufficient to give rise to jurisdiction in the court in which the writ is returnable.

Tort Claim - Non-Resident
1. Defendant is a non-resident.
2. Plaintiff has a just cause against the defendant.
3. The amount of the claim is sufficient to give rise to the jurisdiction of the court in which the writ is returnable.

SOUTH CAROLINA
1. Defendant is a non-resident or a foreign corporation.
2. Defendant is a master, captain, or agent of any sailing vessel entering any port of the state and is about to take such vessel out of said port without paying pilotage fees.

CHART IV (continued)

SOUTH CAROLINA (continued)

3. Defendant has departed the state with the intent to defraud creditors or to avoid service of summons or keeps himself concealed for such purpose.
4. Defendant has removed or is about to remove his property from the state with the intent of defrauding creditors.
5. Defendant has assigned, disposed or secreted his property or is about to do so with the intent of defrauding creditors.

SOUTH DAKOTA

1. Defendant is a non-resident or corporation which can't be served.
2. Defendant departed, removed, secreted, incumbered, transferred or disposed of property with the intent of defrauding creditors.
3. The debt was fraudulently contracted.
4. The action is one for the purchase price of personal property.

TENNESSEE

1. Defendant is a non-resident.
2. Defendant is about to or has removed himself or property from the state.
3. Defendant removed or is about to remove himself from the county.
4. Defendant conceals himself to avoid service.
5. Defendant absconded or is concealing property.
6. Defendant fraudulently disposed of property or is about to do so.
7. The claim is against a non-resident decedent leaving property in the state.

CHART IV (continued)

TEXAS
1. The debt is due for property obtained under false pretenses where seller relied upon the false pretenses as true and so parted with his property.
2. Defendant is a non-resident or foreign corporation.
3. Defendant secretes himself or is about to remove himself from the state.
4. Defendant has secreted his property with the intent of defrauding creditors, or is about to dispose or convert said property with that intent.

UTAH
1. Defendant is a non-resident or foreign corporation not qualified to do business in the state.
2. Defendant can't be served.
3. Defendant assigned, disposed of, or concealed property with intent to defraud creditors, or is about to do so.
4. Defendant departed or is about to depart the state.
5. The debt was fraudulently contracted.
6. When plaintiff can show probable cause of being apprehensive of losing his claim unless attachment issues.

VERMONT
No specific grounds, any action or tort.

VIRGINIA
1. Defendant is a foreign corporation or a non-resident.
2. The defendant is removing or about to remove property from the state.
3. Defendant is converting or about to convert property to hinder, delay, or defraud creditors.

CHART IV (continued)

VIRGINIA (cont'd.)

4. Defendant has assigned or disposed of, or is about to assign or dispose of his property.
5. Defendant has or is about to abscond from the state.
6. Defendant has or is about to conceal himself.
7. Defendant is a fugitive from justice.

WASHINGTON

1. Defendant is a foreign corporation.
2. Defendant is a non-resident.
3. Defendant conceals himself to avoid service of summons.
4. Defendant has absconded or absented himself from his usual place of abode to avoid service of summons.
5. Defendant has removed or is about to remove property with the intent of delaying or hindering creditors.
6. Defendant has assigned, secreted, or disposed of property or is about to do so with the intent of defrauding, hindering or delaying creditors.
7. Defendant has converted his property to money.
8. Defendant fraudulently contracted the debt or obligation.
9. The damabes sought in the suit are for injuries arising from the commission of some felony or for the seduction of some female.
10. The object for which the action is brought is to recover on a contract, express or implied.

WEST VIRGINIA

1. Defendant is a foreign corporation or a non-resident.

CHART IV (continued)

WEST VIRGINIA (continued)

2. Defendant left or is about to leave with intent to defraud creditors.
3. Defendant conceals himself.
4. Defendant is removing, disposing of or converting property with intent of hindering or delaying creditors.
5. Defendant assigned or concealed property with intent to defraud creditors.
6. The debt was fraudulently contracted.

WISCONSIN

1. Defendant is absent from the state or concealed.
2. Defendant is a domestic corporation whose officers cannot be found.
3. Defendant disposed of or concealed property with intent to defraud creditors.
4. Defendant removed property from the state with intent to defraud creditors.
5. The debt was fraudulently contracted.
6. Defendant is a foreign corporation or non-resident.
7. Defendant, as a public officer, defaulted on an official bond.

WYOMING

1. Defendant is a foreign corporation or non-resident.
2. Defendant absconded, left the county or concealed himself to avoid service.
3. Defendant removed, converted, assigned, concealed, or disposed of property with intent to defraud creditors, or is about to do so.
4. The debt was fraudulently contracted.
5. The action is on a contract, express or implied, for the direct payment of money not exceeding $1,500, which contract is unsecured or inadequately secured.

Constitutionality

The Supreme Court has, on several occasions, reviewed various state attachment laws. As previously discussed, the Supreme Court has not held attachments to be unduly oppressive as they did prejudgment garnishments in the Sniadach case.

In 1928, the Supreme Court in the case of Coffin Bros. v. Bennett, 277 U.S. 29, upheld a Georgia statute which authorized the superintendent of banks of that state to levy execution against shareholders of insolvent banks. The statute allowed such attachment when these shareholders had notice, but failed to pay assessments on their stock which assessments were needed to bring the bank back into a state of solvency. These attachments, made before final judgment was rendered, did not deprive the defendant shareholders of their right to raise any defense they may have had in the final hearing of the case. The court ruled, therefore, that the defendants had not been deprived of their constitutional rights of due process.

A similar decision was rendered by the Supreme Court in Ewing v. Mytinger & Cassell Berry, Inc., 339 U.S. 594 (1950) as the court reasoned that prejudgment attachments were merely the statutory prerequisites to bringing the action and not a deprivation of property without due process of law. Contrary to the argument of the defendants, the court reasoned that prejudgment attachments did not deprive the defendants of a full and fair hearing on the merits of the plaintiff's claim.

Courts have consistently recognized the need for such an extreme remedy as prejudgment attachments when the circumstances warranted it. In Fahey v. Mallonee, 382 U.S. 245 (1947), the Supreme Court allowed a Federal agency to take possession of a Federally chartered savings and loan association prior to final hearing on charges levied against the administration of the association that they had been guilty of misconduct. The circumstances warranting the invocation of the extreme remedy were that there appeared no other way to protect the interests of the depositors and investors of the association.

State courts, too, have consistently upheld the validity and constitutionality of their attachment laws, although jealously guarding their application. Courts have long recognized that attachments do not represent a final taking of a debtor's property, but rather only create a lien upon the property which can be available to the creditor after final judgment has been obtained. The process secures to the creditor a fund out of which he may be satisfied after he has successfully proved the validity of his claim.

Grounds

Before a writ or order of attachment can be issued, the court considering the issuance of the order must be convicned that the creditor has stated adequate grounds. That is, the court must ascertain that the circumstances surrounding the claim are such as they comply strictly with the statutory grounds which must be set forth before attachment orders can issue.

1. Nonresidents

Most statutes contain provisions for the attachment of property of debtors who are not residents of the state but have or possess property within the state. When such statutes speak of "persons" being nonresidents, that term is often construed so as to include foreign corporations. A foreign corporation is one that has been organized and exists under and by virtue of the laws of a state other than in which the attachment is sought. For example, a corporation organized in the state of Delaware, but doing business in New York, is a foreign corporation as far as any proceeding in the state of New York is concerned.

The burden of establishing that a defendant is a nonresident or that a corporation is a foreign corporation is upon the plaintiff creditor seeking to invoke the attachment process. He must establish, to the satisfaction of the court, that the defendant debtor does not maintain a residence within the jurisdiction of the court. That is, that he has no abode or home where he may be served personally with summons or other process within the territorial jurisdiction of the court.

Confusion often arises between the terms domicile and residence. Domicile is one's fixed place of habitation. A person's domicile has been construed to mean, that place where he intends to return after any absence, while residence may be something of a more temporary nature. Most state statutes relating to the service of summons allow a defendant to be served at his principal place of residency. The test, then, for nonresidency under the attachment statutes is basically whether or not the debtor has a principal place of residency within the state where he can be served with summons. If the plaintiff creditor can show the court that the debtor has no such place within the state, the attachment order may issue.

A debtor's place of business does not establish his residency, but it may be an element in the proof in determining residency. Other factors to be considered in determining residency include the length of time the debtor has been in the state, his intention to make a particular location his permanent residency, the purpose of his stay in a particular place, the location of his family, and where he exercises his right to vote.

2. Fraudulent Transfers or Attempts to Conceal

Once the ground of nonresidency has been considered, the remaining most prevalent grounds can be grouped together in two main categories. The first is that the defendant debtor has absconded from the jurisdiction or so conceals himself that he cannot be served with process. The second is that the defendant debtor has or is about to remove, conceal, assign, or dispose of his property with the intent of defrauding, hindering, or delaying the creditor from reaching those assets.

Various statutes employ the words "secrete" and "convey" in addition to those mentioned above when speaking of a debtor's intent to put assets beyond the reach of creditors. The most important term employed in such statutes is "intent." No matter the characterization of the act the debtor does, it is imperative in most statutes that it be done with the intent to injure the creditor in his quest for satisfaction of his claim.

Intent, though a nebulous term, can usually be implied from fact and circumstances. The conduct of the debtor is customarily the decisive factor in determining the intent of the debtor. Where intent is a necessary element in the particular statute, it usually can be inferred. What must be considered, then, are the circumstances under which a debtor assigns, transfers, conveys, disposes, removes, or conceals property. It can reasonably be assumed that a debtor who is heavily indebted and converts personal or real property into cash has done so with the intent of putting such property and funds out of the reach of creditors, or defrauding such creditors. Likewise, a debtor who assigns or transfers title to property after incurring debts can be presumed to have done so with the intent of defrauding his creditors.

There are state statutes which, though not necessarily interwoven with attachment procedures, make certain transactions by a debtor fraudulent as a matter of law. For instance, an insolvent debtor who transfers his property is normally presumed to have committed a fraudulent act as it pertains to his creditors. A similar result may be available when an insolvent debtor incurs additional obligations for the purpose of engaging in business. The term "assign" is almost self-explanatory. It refers to the transfer of property, real or personal, or rights connected to such property from one person to another. For instance, a debtor might assign his interest in a lease or mortgage to a third person so that payments thereunder would go to that third person rather than the debtor. Practically speaking, then, the payments due thereunder would be out of the reach of creditors who seek to invoke the normal processes of execution.

The term "secrete" means simply to conceal or hide away. In the context of attachment statutes, the term refers to the efforts of a debtor to put property out of the reach of creditors either by physically hiding the asset or putting the title to such asset in another's name.

When a statute speaks of the term "concealment" or the debtor's concealing of assets, it refers to action by the debtor to hide or disguise the asset so that the creditor no longer can reach it by normal processes of execution. To conceal is almost synonymous with secrete and in a legal sense is to hide away assets either by physically concealing them or transferring title to them so that a creditor cannot reach them.

The use of the word "dispose" in any of the attachment statutes usually pertains to an attempt by the creditor to alienate or direct the ownership of his property to someone other than himself or the creditor. Generically, the term refers to parting with or relinquishing physical property or title thereto.

It can readily be seen that the terms used in the statutes as set forth in Chart IV are all fairly similar in nature. They refer to any attempt or a completed attempt on the part of the debtor to deal with his property in such a manner as to put such property beyond the reach of creditors who, absent such dealings on the part of the debtor, could reach these assets by the use of the normal execution processes of garnishment or judicial sale. Again, it is important to reiterate that the intent of the debtor in dealing with his property is a primary factor to be considered when a creditor seeks to invoke attachment proceedings under those statutes requiring intent on the part of the debtor. Intent can only be manifested by acts and conduct. It is the debtor's purpose or design as measured by the acts that he does which gives rise to an inference of his intent.

Most of the statutes have been construed in such a manner as to allow attachment even though the debtor has not been successful in his attempts to assign, transfer, conceal, dispose of, or remove property. All that is necessary is a showing that the debtor has intended to do so and has taken certain steps under circumstances indicating that he has made an attempt to place such property beyond the reach of creditors.

3. Attempts to Avoid Service

The grouping of grounds which speaks of a debtor's attempts to, or his successful acts of removing himself from the jurisdiction of the court or concealing himself, or absconding, to avoid service are basically self-explanatory. As previously mentioned, the purpose behind the attachment proceeding is to allow the court to obtain jurisdiction over the action when the defendant debtor cannot be served with process in the normal sense of the word.

Since attachment is a prejudgment procedure, in its absence, and in the absence of the defendant upon which to obtain service, the court would have no jurisdiction to entertain the creditor's claim. When a debtor has absconded or removed himself from the jurisdiction of the court so that he cannot be served by mail or by personal service within the territorial jurisdiction of the court, the only recourse a creditor has is to obtain jurisdiction by attachment. That is, the court obtains jurisdiction over the property of the defendant within its territorial jurisdictions and can at least adjudicate a claim in favor of the creditor in the amount of the property within its jurisdiction.

Obviously, if a debtor could defeat a creditor by simply removing himself from the jurisdiction of a court, a creditor would be without recourse except to follow the debtor wherever he might go. The purpose of attachment, then, is to allow a creditor to maintain an action in the forum in which the debtor previously resided and had property, out of which the claim, if adjudicated finally in favor of the creditor, could be satisfied.

Temporary absence from the state or local jurisdiction for either personal or business purposes is not sufficient absence for invoking attachment procedures. Some states provide attachment remedies when the defendant is a fugitive from justice and in such cases, he may not have left the state but most likely cannot be served with process as he conceals his whereabouts for obvious reasons.

If a creditor can establish to the satisfaction of the court that the debtor is about to remove himself from the jurisdiction or about to abscond, or about to conceal himself, the creditor is entitled to an attachment order. The debtor's intention must be to leave without anticipating a return.

4. Fraudulent Debt

A common ground found in many of the state statutes is that the debt was fraudulently contracted or that the obligation was incurred under false pretenses so as to indicate that the debtor in some way misrepresented himself to the creditor. This ground is based primarily on the customary grounds of fraud. That is, the debtor must have made a false representation of a material fact to the creditor upon which he relied in extending credit to the debtor or upon which he relied in releasing goods or services to the debtor. The debtor must have known that he was making a false representation and the creditor must have incurred some damage as a result of relying on the misrepresentation. The important element here is that the debtor intended the misrepresentation to be made and reasonably knew or should have know that the creditor would rely on it in completing the transaction.

Simply because a debtor defaults on a contract does not give rise to a presumption that the debt or obligation was fraudulently incurred. The debtor must have intended not to perform the contract at the time it was executed or entered into before the creditor can rely on that ground for obtaining an order or writ of attachment.

A similar and closely related ground which exists in some states is the giving of a materially false financial statement. Normally a financial institution will require a prospective debtor to list his assets and liabilities so that there can be a reasonable estimation of his ability to pay. If the statement given is materially false and the creditor relies upon it in extending credit, the debt has been fraudulently contracted. While most states incorporate the giving of a false financial statement into the ground that the debt was fraudulently contracted, there are a few which list it as a separate and distinct ground.

5. Other Grounds

Other common grounds include claims for the purchase price of goods delivered to the debtor, or services rendered to him at his request. In this type of action there need not be the usual elements of fraud or attempted fraud. It is sufficient that the creditor supplied goods or services and the debtor has failed to pay for them.

Debts that were incurred by the use of criminal means can normally be secured by the use of attachment. In that vein, many states provide that any damages incurred as a result of the debtor's seduction of any female may be the subject of the primary suit and such may be instituted by attachment.

Levy of Attachment

The procedure for the initiation of the attachment proceeding has already been reviewed. However, we have not yet considered the actual process of physical or constructive attachment. In theory, the appropriate officer of the court, be he a bailiff or sheriff, is to physically take the assets from the debtor's possession once the writ or order has been issued. Possession of the property should remain with that office until the primary suit has been determined. If the creditor, plaintiff, is successful, the property will be turned over to him or sold and the proceeds given to him. If, however, the debtor is the successful party, the property will be returned to him.

Often there arises the problem of how to attach particular types of property. One, of course, cannot take actual physical possession of real property, and often the assets are too bulky or cumbersome to remove. In other instances, the property attached may be perishable and to take possession of them and store them for the time it takes for the court to decide the merits of the primary suit, would cast an undue hardship on both parties to the suit.

In theory, again, the basis of a lien created by attachment is the same as is the basis of any lien -- possession. If the officer who attached the property were to give it up voluntarily, the lien would be lost. Since not all assets can be physically taken and held for the duration of the main suit, most state statutes allow a constructive attachment of certain assets.

Real property, for example, can remain in the possession of and under the control of the debtor after attachment, so long as the lien has been duly noted and announced by the officer of the court levying such attachment. Often, assets consisting of personal property are left in the debtor's possession after attachment. The debtor himself or some third person may be appointed as custodian of the property and charged with the responsibility of safeguarding it until after the primary suit has been determined.

Once the officer of the court has made his attachment, either actual or constructive, he must make a report or return to the court. He must specify the goods collected, the person who has been appointed custodian, if any, and the value of the property taken. Most statutes require that the creditor post a bond when initiating the attachment procedure and often the amount of that bond is dependent on the value of the goods attached. If it is necessary, an appraisal of the goods might be ordered for that purpose.

Wrongful Attachment

Although every possible precaution is taken by the courts in issuing attachment orders, it is possible that the attachment might still be wrongful. The creditor, although required to file an affidavit that certain grounds for the attachment exist, might be mistaken or even purposefully untruthful.

A debtor whose assets are attached may judicially question the validity of the attachment. Usually if the creditor can show probable cause for making the allegations in the affidavit, he will prevail in that particular part of the action. If he cannot, he may find himself subject to liability in one of two ways.

If the creditor was required to file a bond upon beginning the attachment and the statute so permits it, the creditor's liability might be limited to the amount of the bond. Otherwise, the debtor might bring what amounts to a malicious prosecution suit.

A suit in malicious prosecution requires that the debtor show that he was the successful party in the action which determined the validity of the attachment. Further, the debtor must usually show that the attachment was brought by the creditor maliciously and without probable cause. He must further show that he has been damaged in some respect. Most states require a wrongful sequestration of property or arrest of the person before the court will entertain such a suit. In the case of wrongful attachment, there has been a sequestration of property and if the debtor can establish malice on the part of the creditor, he has a good chance of being successful in this type of case. Even though the creditor eventually prevails in the primary suit against the debtor, the attachment may still be wrongful if adequate grounds for such did not exist. Further, if the creditor relied upon a certain ground which turned out to be untrue, he may still be liable for wrongful attachment even though the debtor had acted in such a way so as to subject him to attachment on another ground.

The particulars of such suits vary from state to state. Some states require a showing of malice on the part of the creditor; others do not. Some require a showing of a lack of probable cause; others do not. Where malice is a necessary element of the suit, the creditor might defend on the basis that he relied upon the advice of his attorney. This would tend to mitigate the charge of malice.

When a debtor brings his action upon the bond filed by the creditor, he must look to the statute to determine his rights and extent of damages recoverable. Normally such statutes allow the debtor to recover any and all damages which he sustained as a proximate result of the wrongful attachment. This would include depreciation of the property, damage to the property and the like. Many statutes permit the debtor to further recover his attorney fees which were necessitated by the wrongful attachment and the court costs connected therewith.

Apart from statutory allowances of damages, the debtor is permitted recovery of any damages which naturally flowed from the wrongful attachment or malicious prosecution. Such damages would include the value of the goods at the time they were taken, if they were later lost or destroyed. If the goods were damaged, this amount would probably be recoverable. Depending on the jurisdiction involved, other elements might be the loss of profits or injury to business created by the attachment, injury to credit rating, or even mental suffering caused by the wrongful suit.

The damages above mentioned are those which attempt to place the debtor back in the position he was prior to the suit. They compensate him for his actual losses and make him whole. These are compensatory damages.

Beyond compensatory damages, a debtor might be entitled to punitive damages. Punitive damages are usually available when the attachment was done willfully, maliciously and without probable cause. In other words, the attachment was issued for the sole purpose of harrassing the debtor. Punitive damages are those damages awarded as a punishment against the wrongdoer, and in theory act as a deterrent against further wrongdoing.

A debtor whose property has been taken wrongfully is not, then, without recourse. A further protection is afforded him in the way of exemption statutes even though the attachment is rightful.

Depending upon the state in which the attachment procedure is initiated, the procedure may be thought of as one that is extraordinary in nature or very routine. In those states which allow it in any type of action and without the necessity of formal grounds, it is just another procedural requirement to be met. In those states which recognize its extraordinary nature, it is a procedure whose use must be judiciously guarded.

Chapter Six

EXEMPTIONS FROM ATTACHMENT

Generally

Exemption can generally be defined as a right given to a debtor by law to retain a certain portion or specified items of property free from execution, sequestration or judicial sale by his creditors.

Every state has either by constitutional provision or by statute, exempted certain property from levy of execution. The statutes to be discussed apply generally to all types of legal process whereby a creditor attempts to satisfy his claims from the property of the debtor. That is, no matter if the creditor chooses garnishment, attachment, foreclosure, or judicial sale of personal property, the exemption statutes must be consulted to determine what property will be protected.

Although the exemptions granted vary from state to state, each state has constitutional exemptions or has enacted statutes pursuant to constitutional authority to protect the basic subsistence of the debtor. State legislatures are, of course, bound to act within the limits established by the constitution.

It is not hard to understand the underlying reason for the passage of exemption provisions. Just as Congress found need for large wage exemptions in its Consumer Credit Protection Act, state legislatures and framers of state constitutions found a need to protect debtors from total destitude as a result of creditor collections practices. A debtor should not be deprived of the necessities of life. Not only would such a debtor be in a position of economic disaster, but probably would become dependent upon society for his very existence. Thus, both the public in general and the debtor in particular benefit from exemption statutes. Unfortunately many of the states have not revised their exemption laws to conform with what is realistic in today's society. Perhaps there will be forthcoming uniform exemption statutes or federal legislation, as has been the case of wage garnishments, to bring these antiquated state statutes up to acceptable standards.

An Iowa court has said that it is better to have a creditor go unsatisfied than to deprive a debtor and his dependents of what is essential for their education, culture and spiritual upbuilding. On the other hand, exemption statutes meant to be a shield in the hands of a debtor should not be used as a sword. They should not be employed in such a way to evade payments to creditors. With the spirit of these laws in mind, let us look at some of the legal technicalities of such statutes.

Legal Aspects

Since exemption laws did not exist at common law and are strictly statutory, they must be construed in accordance with the general principles of statutory construction. They should be interpreted liberally in favor of the persons they were designed to protect, i.e., debtors whose property has been subjected to legal process.

Without examining the particular statutes at this point, many statutes specify certain persons who are to be protected by their application to the exclusion of all other persons. The first determination, then, is whether the debtor seeking protection under the statute is a member of the class of persons designated by the statute. This might not be as easy a decision to make as it first appears. For instance, what persons fall within the definitions of laborers, mechanics, farmers, or heads of households?

A mechanic, for example, has been defined to be a skilled workman employed in shaping materials such as wood, metal, or stone into some kind of structure or machine or other object requiring the use of tools. This definition would seem to exclude the person who repairs automobiles or other intricate pieces of machinery, commonly referred to as a mechanic.

Mechanic used in another state's exemption statute has been taken to mean any person who works with machines or with instruments. Judicial interpretation of this latter statute resulted in the extension of the definition to include such varied occupations as bakers, barbers, dentists, or even tailers, not to mention those persons who we commonly refer to as mechanics.

Those vested with the responsibility of providing the support and amintenance of a spouse, children or other dependents are deliniated as a special classification in many exemption laws and are called such varied names as head of a family, head of the household, or householder. These terms, although very similar on their face, have been given many various definitions, and include or exclude persons depending upon the interpretations made under the particular statute.

Whether it is necessary that the person claiming the head of household exemption actually has some legal obligation to support other persons as opposed to a moral obligation to do so has been decided both ways under various court interpretations. On the other side of the coin, what of the person who has a legal obligation to support but does not do so?

There cannot, of course, be a head of the household without a family, but what constitutes a family? A family can be and has been defined as a collective body of persons living in one house and under one head or manager and includes those who reside with or compose the household.

A family, then, can be thought of in the normal sense of the word, rather than some legal technical meaning; and must, of course, be something more than a temporary arrangement among strangers. However, the debtor seeking the exemption as head of the household need not be married, in most states, to qualify. The qualifications are met when a person is responsible for the support and maintenance of relatives with whom he lives. A son may be the head of the household when he resides with his parents and provides the majority of their support.

Although one normally thinks of the husband and father as being the one, rather than the wife, who would qualify for the head of the household exemption, there may be situations where the opposite is true. If the husband is absent from the household forr one reason or another, or is incapacitated and unable to support the family, the wife may qualify for the exemption. She must be the one supporting the family, and must be doing so out of necessity. In no case can both the husband and wife claim the exemption successfully. Only one such exemption, be it for wages or property, is extended to each family unit. Head of the household exemptions may also be extended to divorced men who are legally responsible for the support and maintenance of the ex-wife and minor children, and such exemptions may be extended to widows or widowers depending on the facts and circumstances and the particular statute involved.

Some states have interpreted their head of the household exemption statutes as implying a support and maintenance situation by a parent. A debtor who supported his widowed mother and invalid brother was found not to be a head of the household in the absence of a parent-child relationship.

Some states do not require any obligation of support to qualify the debtor for a head-of-the-household exemption. The statute's foundation is that in any household there should be one person entitled to the exemption, and there need not even be a family. Under such a statute, it was determined that a married woman living apart from her husband and having no child with her was entitled to a head-of-the-household exemption for herself when she was receiving no support from her husband.

The possibilities of interpretation under each of the state's exemption statutes is endless. Basically, however, it is important to remember that such statutes confer a right or privilege to a qualified person, and such right or privilege is personal and cannot be transferred.

We have already discussed the meaning of residency in connection with attachments, but it also becomes important when considering the avialability of exemption statutes to particular individuals. Some states differentiate between residents and nonresidents in applying their exemption statutes.

The general weight of authority has held that if the statute does not specifically deliniate between residents and nonresidents, that every person must be given equal protection under the exemption law.

Residency is largely dependent upon the debtor's intention in making the state in question his home. Intention, although a rather nebulous test for determining anything, can be determined from the acts and conduct of the debtor. Temporary absence from his residency will not, as we have already seen, destroy the residency qualification needed to take advantage of an exemption statute requiring such.

Homestead Exemption

A homestead exemption puts beyond reach of creditors a debtor's residence or a specified portion of it. The exemption is given not for the benefit of the debtor, but rather for the protection of the debtor's family and in part for the protection of the public which might be otherwise burdened with the support of such insolvent debtor.

Many states provide that any resident of the state may qualify for the exemption. Other states allow the exemption to residents who are owners and users of the premises sought to be exempt if the premises is truly his place of abode. Some states extend the exemption to only heads of households or to aged or infirmed persons. Ohio, for example, provides that the exemption will only be available to a husband and wife living together, or to a widow or widower living with an unmarried daughter or minor son. Georgia extends the exemption to a head of a family, an aged or infirmed person, or one who has the responsibility of caring for a dependent female of any age.

The most prevalent restrictions are that one be a resident of the state and the head or financial head of the family.

While the persons qualified for the exemption are somewhat standardized among states, the size of the exemption varies greatly from state to state. Maryland has no such exemption while Nevada allows a ten thousand dollar exemption so long as the claim on which enforcement is sought is not one for the purchase price of the property or on a mortgage on the premises entered into by both the husband and wife.

Some states measure their exemption by acreage rather than dollar value, while others use a combination of the two. Some states differentiate between land located in urban and rural districts. North Dakota, for example, sets the exemption at two acres in a town plot while 160 acres may be exempt in other districts. Oregon's statute is interesting in that it sets a seven thousand dollar maximum on exempted property and an area limitation of not more than one block in any town or city and not more than 160 acres elsewhere.

Many states require a declaration of homestead to be filed and recorded with the appropriate official before the homestead exemption can be considered. Nevada, typical of these states, requires filing of the declaration of homestead with the county recorder in which the property is located.

Like Maryland, Indiana has no homestead exemption statute, but does exempt real property from levy of execution or other process up to a value of seven hundred dollars. Maryland lumps its real property exemption together with the personal property exemptions, and the debtor can select five hundred dollars worth of real or personal property as being exempt.

Iowa provides an exception to its statute. Normally, one-half acre in a city or town plot, or forty acres in a rural district will be exempt. If, however, all other non-exempt property has been taken and the debt not yet satisfied, the homestead may be taken if the debt was contracted prior to the acquisition of the homestead. Likewise, if the debt was entered into and evidenced by a written contract waiving the homestead exemption, or if the debt represents work or materials supplied for improvement of the homestead, the exemption may be lost.

The foregoing only serves to alert the reader of the tremendous divergence between states in how they apply their homestead exemptions. Obviously, the majority of states do not provide sufficient protection to a debtor to adequately protect his home from judicial sale or other process. When homesteads are sold by such process, the amount exempted will be put aside and the remainder will go to the creditor.

The Consumer Credit Protection Act, which has been referred to so often herein, in a way sought to protect the homesteads of the consuming public. Under that Act a creditor may not have a potential debtor sign a promissory note which upon being reduced to judgment would result in a lien upon his principal place of residence without making such transaction a rescindable one. That is, if the note does not expressly waive the creditor's right to have a lien on the debtor's principal place of residence, the debtor has three business days after the completion of the transaction to cancel it. Since a rescindable transaction is not one that the average seller of automobiles, furniture, and the like can live with, the result of this legislation has been the waiver of a right of lien by most such dealers. The Consumer Credit Protection Act places such a burden on the seller when the transaction is rescindable that most such transactions in the area of consumer goods no longer can result in the loss of the debtor's place of residence.

In an effort to equalize the exemptions available to all persons, some states have extended an additional personal property exemption to those persons who cannot qualify for a homestead exemption. Ohio gives an additional five hundred dollar exemption of real or personal property, to be selected by the debtor, in kieu of the homestead exemption to any person not being able to take advantage of the homestead exemption. That statute interestingly enough specifically excludes passenger cars from exemption.

Although the homestead exemption is an important one, the exemptions which most often come into use either in garnishment, attachment, or even bankruptcy proceedings are those pertaining to personal property. These will be considered next.

Personal Property Exemptions

Typical personal property exemption statutes exempt from levy of execution or other judicial process such items as wearing apparel, tools and implements used by the debtor in his trade or business, household furnishings to a certain extent, livestock, books and pictures, and food.

The persons entitled to those exemptions and the particular items included in the exemptions, of course, vary from state to state. Like the wage exemption statutes, most property exemption statutes allow a greater exemption to persons who are charged with the responsibility of supporting a family.

Ohio's exemption statute is exemplative of many others. Wearing apparel to be selected by the debtor is exempt in an amount not exceeding one hundred dollars in value. Tools and implements for carrying on the debtor's profession, trade or business including agriculture are exempt up to two hundred dollars in value. If the debtor is the head of a family or a widow, the exemption includes all wearing apparel for his family, beds, bedsteads, bedding, one cooking stove and pipe, one stove and pipe used for warming the swelling, and enough fuel for sixty days. Livestock and household furnishings are exempt up to five hundred dollars in value. All books and family pictures are exempt. The tool and implement exemption is raised to five hundred dollars for such head of the family debtors and they are given provisions, free from execution, in an amount not to exceed fifty dollars in value.

New York exempts all wearing apparel, household goods, tools and implements of trade or business up to a value of six hundred dollars along with certain other specified items to the householder or woman. A single male has a similar exemption which, however, does not include household furnishing and is limited to four hundred and fifty dollars.

An examination of the state statutes leads one to believe that they are, for the most part, antiquated and essentially worthless in that they do not protect a debtor from economic disaster in terms of the minimum requirements of life in today's economy. Most statutes, for example, set the maximum exemptions for clothing and household goods at such a low figure that no one could possibly make do with that amount of clothing or furniture. Fortunately, most creditors, at least within this writer's experience, do not look to the personal items of a debtor and his family to satisfy outstanding obligations.

Tools and Implements

The majority of state exemption statutes provide that a debtor may keep a specified portion of his tools and implements used in his profession, trade or business. The statute might also employ the words "instruments, apparatus, materials, or stock in trade" in describing those items which are exempt from process. The purpose of this particular exemption is to allow the debtor to continue in his business in order to generate enough income to support himself and family in the future.

Just what is covered by this exemption is determined by judicial interpretation of the particular statute involved. The statute may be worded in such a manner to limit the exemption to those items which are absolutely necessary for the debtor to continue his business, or the statute may imply that those items which are reasonably necessary for that purpose may be selected by the debtor.

Under the Ohio statute, for example, the law library of an attorney along with his office furnishings have been held to be tools and implements of his profession, and therefore exempt. The automobile of a physician was held to be an implement of his profession and exempt, but the autos of a real estate broker and of an electrician we e held non-exempt as not being necessary for trade or business.

Implements used by a farmer may be exempt under the trade or business portion of the exemption statutes, or may be excluded under a portion of the statute directed specifically at farmers. Idaho, for instance, has a specific exemption allowing farmers to keep farming utensils not exceeding three hundred dollars in value.

Those statutes containing special exemptions for agriculture must be construed to determine who qualifies and what activities constitute being in the business of agriculture. In one reported case, a person living in a village and cultivating corn, potatoes, cabbage, beans and the like on two town lots containing less than one-half acre was found not to be one engaged in the business of agriculture. This does not mean that in another jurisdiction an opposite result may not have been obtained. The latitute of interpretations is that wide.

Beyond the mere tools and implements of trade or business, some statutes exempt a specified portion of materials or stock in trade employed by the debtor in his business. Others include an automobile or other vehicle similarly employed, while still others expressly include professional libraries and other books.

The questions of interpretation are endless. Does equipment fall within an exemption for tools and implements? Do the instruments of a dentist or doctor fall within the scope of a statute exempting only tools? We could go on infinitum asking and answering such questions. Suffice it to say that it is up to the courts in the state whose law is being tested to determine the answers to these questions.

Household Goods and Wearing Apparel

Most states exempt certain household furnishings and wearing apparel to a certain extent. The particular statute may either enumerate the items to be exempted or provide a general clause whereby the debtor can select the items which he wishes to be exempt. Representative statutes are as follows:

States	Statutes
Alabama	Necessary family clothing.
California	Necessary household furniture.

States	Statutes
Colorado	Wearing apparel not exceeding $250 in value. Household goods up to $750 in value.
Idaho	Chairs, tables, desks up to $200 in value plus certain other household goods and wearing apparel.
Iowa	Wearing apparel, other items plus kitchen not exceeding $200 in value.
Kansas	Furnishings and supplies, clothing and food sufficient for a period of one year.
Maine	Household goods and wearing apparel not exceeding $500 in value.
Massachusetts	Household furniture not exceeding $1,000 in value.
Missouri	Household furniture and wearing apparel not in excess of $200.
Nebraska	Necessary wearing apparel and household goods including kitchen utensils not exceeding $1,000 in value.
New Jersey	$500 worth of personal property.
North Dakota	All wearing apparel of the debtor and his family plus one year's supply of food and fuel for heating.
Oregon	Wearing apparel of not more than $100 in value for the debtor and an additional $50 worth for each member of his family.
Tennessee	Personal property of up to $1,500 in value.

State	Statute
Washington	Household furnishings and utensils not to exceed $1,000 in value, plus $400 worth of other personal property including wearing apparel.

Definitional problems arise in the application of these statutes as we have seen in the case of all other statutes mentioned herein. Household goods, by definition, usually includes everything which may contribute to the use or convenience of the householder or the ornament of the house such as plate, linen, china, pictures and the like.

Many statutes provide that family pictures are exempt. When a statute includes such an item, it contemplates pictures, the subject of which are the family members or taken by the family. Such a statute does not include a private gallery of costly pictures.

Since many of the statutes allow the debtor to select the property which he wants to hold as exempt, and the statute imposes a monetary limit on that property, a problem as to valuation often arises. Many states in contemplation of such problems have provided for the appointment of appraisers in the event no agreement can be reached as to the value of the goods. Other states rely upon the officer of the court levying execution on the goods to make such valuations.

The debtor must make the selection of the goods which he intends to hold as exempt. Until such selection is made and the exemption put into effect, the property is not exempt. There is no presumption in the law that a debtor will choose certain goods as opposed to others. Unlike the exemption for wages under the Consumer Credit Protection Act which is self-executing, an exemption pertaining to property to be selected by the debtor must be exercised by the debtor before it will have any force or effect.

Miscellaneous Features

Some states provide specific exclusions from the exemption laws. Many states do not allow an exemption on particular property when the debt which gave rise to the garnishment, attachment, or other judicial process is a claim for the purchase price of the article which would otherwise be exempt. Some states exclude those debts arising from a mortgage signed by both the husband and wife. Other typical exclusions include claims for manual labor, mechanics liens, and claims arising out of the supplying of labor or materials for the erection of the dwelling house. Likewise, most of the exemption statutes do not cover partnerships, corporations or other entities. They pertain to individual debtors only.

As a general rule, the law in force at the time the debt was contracted and not that in force when suit is brought will govern the extent of the exemptions available to the debtor. Likewise, as a general rule, any attempt by a creditor to have the debtor waive his rights to exemptions at the time the contract for the debt is entered into will be null and void.

Other items exempted by various state statutes include:

Automobiles to a specified value
Bibles
Cemetery lots
Church pew
Cows and pigs
Domestic animals
Drawings and paintings to a specified value
Family keepsakes
House trailer occupied as a swelling to a specified amount
Intangible personal property to a specified value (debts owing to the debtor, etc.)
Jewelry and personal items to a specified amount
Luggage
Mining claim up to a specified value
Musical instruments
Poultry
Refrigerator
School books
Sewing machines

In view of this wide variety of items that can be exempted, a debtor faced with the situation of attachment or other process by which his personal items may be taken, must make himself aware of his particular state's exemptions.

Chapter Seven

CONCLUSION

Consumer protection is the watchword of our times. The tremendous rise in consumer credit has resulted in not only an unparalled standard of living, but also a disastrous rise in personal bankruptcies. Directly attributing to the rise in the bankruptcy rate has been the unfettered use of garnishments to reach the wages of debtors.

Until the enactment of the Consumer Credit Protection Act, each state was solely responsible for the operation of and scope of its garnishment laws. With the enactment of the Consumer Credit Protection Act came some standardization of the amount of personal earnings that could be taken by garnishment process. At least a maximum amount, or a minimum exemption, has been established.

The Consumer Credit Protection Act further sought to protect an employee debtor from losing his employment by reason of the fact that his wages had been subjected to garnishment. Many states followed suit by enacting similar provisions.

Currently, there are several states which have sought to conform their garnishment statutes to the Federal legislation. These states have attempted to exempt their statutes from application of the Federal law by taking advantage of the provision thereof which allows such exemption if the state law is substantially similar to or more restrictive than the Federal statute. To date, no state has been successful in obtaining the exemption. The Administrator of the Wage and Hour Division of the Department of Labor, who is responsible for the administration and policing of the Act, has encountered many problems of interpretation of both the Federal legislation and the statutes of the states seeking exemption. It is anticipated that there will be considerable litigation under all of the new statutes before definitional, arithmetical, and procedural problems are overcome. The Federal legislation has, however, brought the problem of wage garnishments to a head; and it can reasonably be anticipated that the near future will hold an enlightened and economically responsible garnishment posture.

In an indirect way, the Consumer Credit Protection Act has already effectively eliminated prejudgment garnishments. The rationale behind the Federal legislation was extended by the Supreme Court to prejudgment garnishments, and since the Court rendered its opinion in the Sniadach case, several states have complied with said ruling by eliminating prejudgment garnishments.

Beyond wage garnishments, a debtor may be faced with attachment of his property or garnishment of his property in the hands of another.

The Supreme Court has consistently upheld the extraordinary remedy of attachment before judgment when the circumstances warrant it. Unlike wage garnishment, the individual states still have exclusive control of and direction over attachment procedures. Each state has established certain grounds or classes of cases in which the attachment remedy may be used. Several states still regard the process of attachment as merely a means by which an action may be instituted. It may be considered as a process whereby a court obtains jurisdiction to hear the primary suit where it would be otherwise impossible to acquire jurisdiction because the defendant is not available to be served personally.

Property which may be taken by either attachment or garnishment of other than wages is limited by the application of exemption statutes. Exempt property varies from state to state, but each state has tried to leave a debtor with the bare necessities of life. In many respects, however, these statutes are inadequate and must be revised to meet the purpose for which they were intended.

Obviously, a creditor who has sold goods or services, or lent money in good faith, is entitled to be paid. On the other hand, a debtor who is not able to pay should not be subjected to undue harrassment or total deprivation of his property. Such tactics can only leand to bankruptcy.

The answer appears to be an orderly, just, and equitable procedure for the collection of debts. State legislatures must begin or, in some instances, continue in their efforts to effectuate this goal. While garnishment of wages has, in a small way, undergone effective change, attachments, garnishment of property other than wages, and exemptions from such processes need revamping.

Until such time as uniform state legislation in all areas is adopted, problems in the nature of those discussed throughout this article will continue.

Consumer protection is by no means a theory of the past. Nor should creditor protection be totally disregarded. It appears that the pendulum has swung from the creditor to the debtor, in some respects, and it is time to scrutinize the total picture of debtor-creditor relations.

Appendix A

THE CONSUMER CREDIT PROTECTION ACT
(effective July 1, 1970)

Restriction on garnishment--Maximum allowable garnishment, Sec. 1672.

(a) Except as provided in subsection (b) of this section and in section 1675 of this title, the maximum part of the aggregate disposable earnings of an individual for any workweek which is subjected to garnishment may not exceed

- (1) 25 per centum of his disposable earnings for that week, or
- (2) the amount by which his disposable earnings for that week exceed thirty times the Federal minimum hourly wage prescribed by section 206(a)(1) of title 29 in effect at the time the earnings are payable,

whichever is less. In the case of earnings for any period other than a week, the Secretary of Labor shall by regulation prescribe a multiple of the Federal minimum hourly wage equivalent to that set forth in paragraph (2).

(b) The restrictions of subsection (a) of this section do not apply in the case of

- (1) any order of any court for the support of any person,
- (2) any order of any court of bankruptcy under chapter XIII of the Bankruptcy Act,
- (3) any debt due for any State or Federal tax.

(c) No court of the United States or any State may make, execute, or enforce any order or process in violation of this section.

Restriction on discharge from employment by reason of garnishment, Sec. 1674.

(a) No employer may discharge any employee by reason of the fact that his earnings have been subject to garnishment for any one indebtedness.

(b) Whoever willfully violates subsection (a) of this section shall be fined not more than $1,000, or imprisoned not more than one year, or both.

Exemption for State-regulated garnishments, Sec. 1675.

The Secretary of Labor may by regulation exempt from the provisions of section 1673(a) of this title garnishments issued under the laws of any state if he determines that the laws of that State provide restrictions on garnishments which are substantially similar to those provided in section 1673(a) of this title.

Enforcement by Secretary of Labor, Sec. 1676.

The Secretary of Labor, acting through the Wage and Hour Division of the Department of Labor, shall enforce the provisions of this subchapter.

Effect on State laws, Sec. 1677.

This subchapter does not annul, alter, or affect, or exempt any person from complying with, the laws of any State

       (1) prohibiting garnishments or providing for more limited garnishments than are allowed under this subchapter, or

       (2) prohibiting the discharge of any employee by reason of the fact that his earnings have been subjected to garnishment for more than one indebtedness.

Appendix B

FEDERAL WAGE GARNISHMENT NOTICE TO BE ATTACHED TO GARNISHMENT ORDER

IMPORTANT NOTICE

The garnishment restrictions of Title III of the Consumer Credit Protection Act (15 U.S.C. 1673) provide that no court of the United States may make, execute, or enforce any order or process which provides for the garnishment of the aggregate disposable earnings of any individual for any workweek in an amount which is in excess of the lesser of the following restrictions:

(1) 25 per cent of the individual's disposable earnings for the workweek, or
(2) the amount by which his disposable earnings for that week exceed 30 times the minimum wage under Section 6(a)(1) of the Fair Labor Standards Act of 1938 (29 U.S.C. 206(a)(1)), which is presently $1.60 an hour.

These restrictions do not apply in the case of (1) Court orders for the support of any person, (2) Court orders under Chapter XIII of the Bankruptcy Act, and (3) Any debt due for any State or Federal Tax.

"Disposable earnings" is compensation paid or payable for personal services less any amounts required to be withheld by law. The law also prohibits an employer from discharging any employee because his earnings have been subjected to garnishment for any one indebtedness. The term "one indebtedness" refers to a single debt, regardless of the number of levies made or creditors seeking satisfaction. Whoever willfully violates the discharge provision of this law may be prosecuted criminally and fined up to $1,000, or imprisoned for not more than one year, or both.

A section or provision of the State law that requires a larger amount to be garnished than the Federal law permits is considered pre-empted by the Federal law. On the other hand, the State law provision is to be applied if it results in a smaller garnishment amount.

Information regarding the Federal Wage Garnishment Law may be obtained from any office of Wage and Hour Division, U.S. Department of Labor.

INDEX

Assignment, wage, 32, 33-38
Attachment
  Definition, 4
  Constitutionality, 90
  General, 68
  Grounds, 70-89; 91
  Levy, 96
  Wrongful, 97
  Exemptions, 100
Bankruptcy Law, 15
Consumer Credit Protection
  Act, 6, 8, 10, 14, 17, 29, 41, 44, 63, 105, 112
Creditors Bill, 61
Concealment, 93
Compensatory Damages, 99
Dispose, 93
Earnings (wages; salary; personal)
  Definition, 15
  Disposable, 16
Exemptions, 5, 44, 100
  Bank account, 49
  Decedents estate, 62
  Equitable interests, 60
  General, 48
  Homestead, 6, 104
  Household goods & wearing apparel, 108-110
  Legal aspects, 101

Exemptions (cont'd.)
  Life insurance, 51, 53-59
  Miscellaneous, 110
  Partnership property, 59
  Pensions, 63
  Real Property, 48
  State chart, 19-26, 38-39
  Stocks, 63
  Tools & implements, 107
Garnishments
  Definition, 2, 17
  Procedure, 64
  Before judgment, 7
  After judgment, 10
Individual, 17
In Rem, 68
Judgment Execution, 11
Labor Relations Act, 12
National Labor Relations Board, 12, 13
Pay Periods, 17
Persona Jurisdiction, 68
Punitive Damages, 99
Quasi Rem Proceeding, 68
Secrete, 93
Trustree Process, 11
Uniform Consumer Credit Code, 18, 28, 46
Uniform Partnership Act, 59
Wage Assignments (chart), 33-38